SIR CHRISTOPHER WREN

SIR
CHRISTOPHER WREN

A Biography

by

HAROLD F. HUTCHISON

READERS UNION
Group of Book Clubs
Newton Abbot 1976

First published by Victor Gollancz Ltd

This edition was produced in 1976 for sale to its members
only by the proprietors, Readers Union Limited,
PO Box 6, Newton Abbot, Devon, TQ12 2DW.
Full details of membership will gladly be sent on request

Reproduced and printed in Great Britain
by A. Wheaton & Co Exeter
for Readers Union

CONTENTS

ILLUSTRATIONS

Between pages 64 and 65

PREFACE

In 1750, Sir Christopher Wren's grandson published a miscellaneous and badly edited collection of the Wren family papers in the volume entitled *Parentalia*. It is still, with all its faults, a major and fascinating source book for Wren's life and family background.

It was not until 1823—a century after Wren's death—that an attempt was made at a complete biography, by James Elmes. Elmes was himself an architect, and, although his professional career was sadly cut short by early blindness, nothing could dim his worship of Wren. Unfortunately, his zeal was undiscriminating, and his facts were unreliable; yet his two volumes on Wren and his times are still invaluable compilations of raw materials and hallowed traditions.

Since 1823, there have been at least twenty books in English devoted to Wren, but most of them have been monographs on Wren as the great architect. It is no exaggeration to maintain that even today few people are fully aware of the fact that Wren was a distinguished professional astronomer until he was in his mid-thirties, and that it was as a scientist and an astronomer that he became a founder-Fellow of the Royal Society.

For the most part, modern monographs have been written by architects or architectural historians for architects or students of architecture. I have, therefore, tried to write the present book for general readers in a language which they can fully understand without having to puzzle over the more abstruse technical terms of the architectural schools, and without having to be proficient in higher mathematics, and I wanted to substantiate my text with helpful reference notes and a serviceable index— it is astonishing that even the best modern monographs on Wren contain neither. And I wanted to do full justice to Wren's background, to his first career as a scientist, and not only to his prodigious work as an architect but to his personality as a lovable and versatile Englishman.

I am indebted to all my predecessors in these aims, but I must pay special tribute to the compilers of that wealth of evidence which is contained in the twenty volumes of the Wren Society. And I must record my special thanks to the encouraging co-operation I have received from the librarians of the Bodleian and of Oxford and Cambridge colleges, Westminster Abbey, St Paul's Cathedral, Salisbury Cathedral, Guildhall, the British Museum, the Soane Museum, and the Royal Society, and especially from Mr David Dean, the librarian of the RIBA. And, once again, I pay tribute to the long-suffering encouragement and secretarial efficiency of my wife.

HAROLD F. HUTCHISON

HOVE, 1975

SIR CHRISTOPHER WREN

I

Backgrounds—1632-49

ON 20 OCTOBER 1632, a somewhat delicate son was born to
the Reverend Dr Christopher Wren and his wife at East Knoyle
—a small village in the rolling countryside of Wiltshire some
sixteen miles west of Salisbury. The father was the well-
connected local rector, and the child was christened Christopher after him. The mother was the daughter and heiress of
one Robert Cox from the neighbouring village of Fonthill. The
new baby was his parents' sixth, and was the only son to survive
infancy—it was an age of large families and heavy infant
mortality.[1] The child was to become the Sir Christopher Wren
who, nearly 91 years later, was to be buried with great state but
in a simple tomb in the crypt of the new cathedral of St Paul's
in London whose planning and designing he had originated,
and whose construction and decoration he had supervised from
start to finish.

It was to be a prodigious life-span which began when England's King and Parliament were drifting into civil war, which
was to see a king beheaded and a dictatorship established,
which was to flourish during the expansive years of the Restoration period, which was to reach its zenith after the Glorious
Revolution of 1688, and which was to be only slightly dimmed
when a Hanoverian dynasty finally took over from the last of
the Stuarts. In what kind of an England did Sir Christopher
Wren begin his very long and very distinguished life, and what
were his domestic and intellectual backgrounds?

Early seventeenth-century England was a small kingdom on the
outer edge of the then civilized world—it was not yet the heart
of an overseas empire. Its total population was about five

million, the bulk of whom lived south of the river Trent, and although there were scores of towns they were all of little consequence when compared with the metropolis of London, whose citizens numbered between a quarter and half a million, and whose wealth and independence made them a social and political force with which Crown and Parliament always had to reckon.

Most Englishmen of the time were still closely connected with the soil—even townsmen had their fields and fisherfolk their crofts. The majority tilled the land or depended on the great flocks of sheep, either as shepherds or as spinners and weavers of wool, or as merchants transporting raw wool or woven cloth to ports and markets. And, although most communities had to be self-sufficing, there were great seasonal fairs where the arts and crafts of the townsfolk and the produce of the country folk could find a ready exchange, and here and there were hints of the industrialization which was still to come. The homes of the ordinary people were thatched wattle-and-daub cottages in the country and overcrowded and insanitary half-timbered houses in the towns. For domestic heating, wood or peat was the fuel in rural areas, while the larger towns were able to obtain "sea-coal", transported by sea and river from the primitive mines of the north. There was a network of roads, some still based on the ancient Roman roads, but they were all quagmires in poor weather and the hunting grounds of high-waymen, and, as neither public coaches nor metalled tracks were yet available, most travellers went on horseback.

England in 1632 was comparatively prosperous and peaceful —there had been no battle fought south of the Border since 1513 when Scotland's King had fallen at the Battle of Flodden in remote Northumberland. Not long before, England had as-tounded Europe by defeating a Spanish Armada, and since then her captains and seamen had earned the growing respect of Portuguese, Spanish, French and Dutch rivals in the new worlds which were being revealed beyond both the western and eastern horizons. It was fortunate too that their victories had been won on foreign soil or the high seas; England had remained inviolate.

Socially, a society of feudal lords who spoke Norman-French and serfs who spoke Anglo-Saxon had been replaced by a society in which all men were free and spoke English, and in which the class barriers were less visible than their continental counterparts. Much of the old nobility had committed suicide in the internecine warfare of the fifteenth century. There was now a new aristocracy whose new country mansions no longer needed to be fortified, and whose new wealth was based partly on the rich trade with the Low Countries and with other overseas territories east and west. True, there were still problems connected with the indigent poor, but since the beginning of the century a Poor Law had begun to tackle them, and both monarchy and aristocracy were bridled by a sturdy free yeomanry in the country and a powerful and rich merchant class in the towns.

In religious affairs, England's Reformation had been skilfully managed so as to avoid the extremisms of the continent. A Protestant State Church had been established of which it could truly be said, in the admirable words of the introduction to its Book of Common Prayer, that "it hath been the custom of the Church of England ever since the first compiling of her Public Liturgy to keep the mean between the two extremes of too much stiffness in refusing and of too much easiness in accepting any variation therefrom". The religious executions and burnings of the Tudor period were now evil memories, and for the moment, only avowed papists were denied freedom of worship. True, the Laudian reforms had given inordinate power to bishops, undue Divine Right to the monarch, and threatened a grim future for obstinate Calvinists; but most Englishmen accepted their new compromising Church establishment with satisfaction. The many holy days of the mediaeval Church had been abolished, but in their place every Sunday throughout the year was a "holiday" for all from both work and play. The rigidity of the new English Sunday, however, was already in force[2]—weekly attendance at church with lengthy sermonizing was obligatory, but that it was not wholly unpleasing the pages of Pepys' and Evelyn's diaries can prove. The clergy were now allowed to marry, but university dons were still expected to remain celibate. And, although a belief in fairies was less widespread, witches, in spite of a growing scepticism, were still persecuted and frequently burned or executed.

There was, of course, no such thing as universal education,

but grammar schools in some of the towns and cities were doing excellent work for all except the very poor. Most tradesmen could read, write and keep their accounts and diaries, while the better educated gentry were fully grounded in Latin and less frequently in Greek. Printing was subject to strict censorship and savage penalties for infringements, but the Bible and the prayer-book were free to all in their superb Jacobean-English versions.

For recreation, there were boisterous and ill-regulated games which included the beginnings of modern stool-ball and cricket. The bowling greens of England were famous, and archery was still officially encouraged. In the country, gentry hunted the deer (and not the fox), and the shooting and snaring of birds and angling for fish were popular sports which were of practical benefit to the domestic economy; while in the towns cock-fighting and bear-baiting were the delight of gamblers from all ranks of society. Horse-racing as a national pastime was soon to begin near the royal country house at Newmarket. In London, until the Cromwellian era decreed otherwise, the Elizabethan theatre and the Jacobean masque had been well established, and there were several companies of travelling players introducing drama to provincial audiences. In the capital especially, the Common Law also provided frequent popular spectacles at the public hangings of criminals, while the Law of Treason presented city crowds with the thrills of public trials, and finally with the awesome and bloody sequences of public disembowellings and executions.

There was no police force, no effective standing army and only the beginnings of a permanent Royal Navy, but there was a general local responsibility for public order and for national military or naval service when the need arose. Gentlemen wore their swords at most times, and always carried pistols when they travelled, while ordinary citizens were no strangers to arms and firearms and their usage. Duelling amongst the gentry had become common, but it was subject to a strict code of "honour", and was soon to be discouraged by legal penalties although it persisted for a century or more.

Constitutionally, one serious problem still defied solution— how could a monarchical system of government continue without degenerating into tyranny, and without outraging those

instincts for liberty and self-government which had been born
in the Middle Ages? It was a problem which was about to result
in a civil war which would cut across all traditional class dis-
tinctions, and which would truly be a war of ideas. When its
conclusion came, England was to be left with a system of
government which would restore a monarchy but limit it by the
control of an aristocracy of wealth which had the means and
the brains to overawe not only a Scottish, a Dutch and a
German monarchy in turn, but the ordinary folk of town and
country for the next 200 years.

The young Christopher Wren was born into an England
where he, his parents and all his nearest relatives were heredi-
tary members of a new-style governing aristocracy.

The young Wren can have had few, if any, memories of his
mother—she died when he was only two—but what is known
of his father suggests that his was an impressive and well-loved
personality whose good influence was considerable. He had
taken his degree in divinity at St John's College, Oxford, and
had been made a Fellow, but his interests and accomplishments
covered wider fields. He had designed a new and stronger
king-posted roof for his church at East Knoyle; its walls still
bear witness to his skill as a craftsman in decorative plaster; his
ingenuity had resulted in the invention of a "serpentine"[3]
which was apparently devised to reduce a river of a mile's
length within the compass of a small orchard and so make
possible a local fishing industry; and his marginal notes in his
copy of Sir Henry Wotton's *Elements of Architecture* (1624) prove
that he was a keen architect, and a keen student and designer
of sundials.[4] Already he had found favour in court circles—in
1628 he had been appointed a chaplain to King Charles I, and
there is evidence that he had received a royal commission to
design a mansion for Charles I's Queen, although it was never
built.[5] Three years after his son's birth, he succeeded his brother
Matthew as Dean of Windsor and Registrar of the Order of
the Garter—a regal appointment. He and his family now moved
to Windsor, and the young Wren's earliest memories must have
been not of Wiltshire but of castle and court. There he met and
came to know Prince Charles Louis,[6] the exiled Elector Palatine

(and brother of Prince Rupert) who was lodged at the deanery while trying to persuade Charles I to intervene on his behalf in the Palatinate, and the royal children may well have been among Wren's playmates. It was, therefore, a very royalist and very High Anglican society in which he spent his earliest boyhood.

Wren's uncle Matthew had left Windsor to become in quick succession Bishop of Hereford, of Norwich, and finally in 1638 of Ely. He was an unusually brave and determined character, and an enthusiastic friend and supporter of Archbishop Laud. It was in this latter capacity that he soon fell foul of the Puritans of the Long Parliament. Later, when Laud was impeached (and subsequently executed) Bishop Matthew Wren was lucky to escape a similar fate. He was sent to the Tower without trial, and was to remain there for eighteen years refusing any compromise with and any mercy from his Roundhead gaolers.

The Wrens were at Windsor for some eight years before the outbreak of the civil war uprooted them, and during that time the young Christopher may have divided his time between Windsor and Great Haseley (eight miles east of Oxford) where his father had been granted the rich living on his appointment to Windsor. We are told in *Parentalia* that "by reason of a tender health"[7] young Wren's early education was entrusted to the private tuition of the Reverend William Shepheard, MA, of whom nothing more is known. And the next unchallenged date in his young life is that in 1650 he became a Gentleman Commoner at Wadham College, Oxford.[8] He was living in very troubled times, and this probably accounts for the fact that the story of his upbringing from the age of nine to the age of seventeen cannot be told with dated precision.

We do know that Dean Wren and his family did not long remain undisturbed at Windsor. In October 1642, one Captain Fogg descended upon the deanery with a posse of Roundhead soldiery, and ransacked it. Fortunately, the Dean had buried some of the rarer treasures of the Garter Order in anticipation, but the Order's records and his own personal belongings were pillaged. Later, a second raid by the regicide Cornelius Holland was to find the buried treasure as well, and all seemed lost.

However, the Dean was able to buy back, at his own considerable expense, some of the record books of the Garter at their
subsequent sale, and he was able to hand them over to the
safekeeping of his son until better times arrived. *Parentalia* adds
the touching note that the old man was also able to recover his
own beloved harpsichord.[9]

Meanwhile, Windsor was clearly no safe place for a royalist
dean and his large family. They evacuated to Bristol—at the
time a royalist stronghold—but in the autumn of 1645 the city
was surrendered to Fairfax by Prince Rupert, and once again
the Wrens were in some danger. Fortunately, Wren's elder
sister Susan had by this time met and married the Reverend
Dr William Holder, who had become the rector of Bletchingdon, a small Oxfordshire village near Bicester. There, after a
brief visit to East Knoyle, the Wren family was at last able to
find security and comparative peace.

Susan Holder was Wren's favourite sister, and in many ways
she took the place of his dead mother. She had some reputation
as a "she-surgeon", and in later years she was successfully to
treat Charles II by poulticing a painful inflammation which his
official doctors had failed to cure. Her husband was a "great
virtuoso"—he was both a musician and a mathematician of distinction, and was later to publish learned works on harmony,
ancient Greek music, the Julian calendar and the elements of
speech. He was reputed to have taught a deaf-mute to talk.
Aubrey, who knew the Wrens and the Holders well, wrote that
at this time the young Christopher was "a youth of a prodigious
inventive Witt, and of whom Dr Holder was as tender as if he
had been his owne Child, who gave him his first Instructions in
Geometrie and Arithmetique".[10]

There is also the authority of *Parentalia* for believing that
"for some short time" Wren was at Westminster School under
the celebrated royalist and disciplinarian Dr Busby,[11] but there
is no other evidence of this and no precise dates. The likelihood
is that Wren was at Westminster after receiving his early educational grounding from Shepheard while his parents were at
Bristol, and that after 1645 he divided his time between the
private tuition of Dr Holder at Bletchingdon and the supervision he was fortunate enough to receive from Dr Charles
Scarburgh in London. Scarburgh was both a surgeon-physician

and a mathematician, and he was later to become the knighted physician to Charles II, James II and Queen Anne. In 1647 the young Wren, in an elegant Latin letter to his father, tells of Scarburgh's kindness, and of how in fact he owed his life to him—he had been cured of a serious illness by him.[12]

It is also quite possible that during this period Wren renewed acquaintance with John Wilkins, an Oxford divine who had been private chaplain to the Elector Palatine at Windsor. Wilkins had later espoused the parliamentary cause, but had retained his many connections with the *virtuosi* of London. And, through Wilkins, the young Wren may also have made useful contacts with Oxford—when he actually went up to Oxford he chose Wadham College of which in 1648 Wilkins had become the Warden, and by then Wren was certainly no stranger to the university and its more adventurous scholars.

But, if Wren's precise movements up to the age of seventeen are impossible to pin down, there is ample evidence of his astonishing activities—mostly in the pages of *Parentalia*. At thirteen "this young mathematician" invented an astronomical instrument which he called his *Panorganum Astronomicum*; he carried out exercises in physics concerning the rising of rivers which were based on some suggestions of his father and which he therefore dedicated to him in Latin verse; he invented a "pneumatic engine" of which there are no details surviving; and he constructed "a peculiar instrument of use in gnomonicks" (sundialling) which he called his *Sciotericum Catholicum* or Universal Sundial. At fifteen, he invented a deaf and dumb language (*cheirologia*) using the hands and fingers for which we have his drawing and his notes; he constructed a weather clock of which again there remains his own drawing, and an instrument for writing in the dark; and under Scarburgh's guidance he wrote a treatise on spherical trigonometry by a new method which, to the doctor's delight, he also engraved on a tiny brass plate.[13] Again with Scarburgh's encouragement, he constructed and modelled in pasteboard the astronomical delineations, and translated into Latin a tract of Oughtred's *Clavis Mathematicae* on geometric dialling which the great mathematician used, and later gracefully acknowledged, in the third edition of his celebrated work published in 1652. There is also a record of Wren's ingenious invention of a reflecting sundial for the ceiling of a room, and a note in Aubrey that he constructed various sundials in various buildings at Bletchingdon.[14] *Parentalia* also says that Wren actually became "an assistant" to Dr Scarburgh in preparing his anatomical experiments, and evidently his skill as a model-maker came in useful—he built pasteboard demonstrations of the actions of the human muscles which Scarburgh used in lectures at Surgeons Hall.[15]

It is a remarkable catalogue of achievement for a youth in his early teens, and his gratitude to his father and to Scarburgh is continually expressed in both English and Latin. Incidentally, the competence with which Dr Busby taught him his Latin can be judged by the felicity and facility of his lengthy Latin verses on the fables of the Zodiac.[16] It is beyond doubt that, by the time Wren went up to Oxford, he was already a good mathematician, a good Latin scholar, an expert in "gnomonicks" and accomplished in astronomy, and that he was already creating some stir among the *virtuosi* of his day.

Wren was fortunate in that he had been so little disturbed by the exigencies of civil war. There was, however, one crisis in his young life which he cannot have relished. In 1647, his father had to face serious charges from Roundhead purists—they suggested that his decorative plaster-work in his church at East Knoyle smacked of papistry. An unpleasant inquisition and enquiry resulted in nothing worse than the Dean receiving censure and losing his living at East Knoyle, but the episode must have saddened his declining years. On the other hand, the Dean was luckier than his brother Matthew in the Tower, and was able to live on undisturbed at Bletchingdon, where he died some eleven years later and was buried in the chancel of the church. Wren was blessed with a father whose abilities were well out of the ordinary.

But who were these *virtuosi* of whom Dr Holder, Dr Scarburgh and Dr John Wilkins were leading examples? The intellectual climate of England in the early seventeenth century demands inspection if this question is to be correctly answered, and Wren's early career fully assessed.

The thinkers and intellectual leaders of the later Middle Ages had been dominated by the principles and teachings of four great men—Aristotle, the pupil of Plato and the tutor of Alexander the Great; Ptolemy, the Alexandrian astronomer and geographer; Galen, the physician to the Emperor Marcus Aurelius; and Saint Thomas Aquinas, the thirteenth-century official philosopher of papal catholicism. The result was a corpus of dogmas of universal application which it was dangerous to question and folly to ignore. The earth was the centre of the universe; the sun, the moon, the planets and the fixed stars circled round it; bodies fell at a rate which was in proportion to their weight; and, of course, the biblical version of the Creation, and the early history of the earth and its inhabitants, had to be accepted without question. But, since the fourteenth century, a movement had flourished which has since been termed the Renaissance. It had begun in Italy as a flowering of the arts of architecture, painting, sculpture and literature, and it had spread to France and northern Europe over the succeeding century and a half. The invention of printing, the availability of Latin as a *lingua franca* for all European scholars, and the results of voyages of exploration and of easier means of communication had all stimulated its progress, yet it is perhaps surprising that its effects on what is today called philosophy and science came after and not before its effects on the arts.

It was Copernicus (1473–1543) who first dared to publicize the belief that the sun was the centre of our universe, although the belief had been anticipated by Aristarchus in ancient Greece. That the earth was spherical had always been accepted by the knowledgeable, but that it was spinning on its own axis and orbiting the sun was a belief which took much longer to take root. Four great scholars (whose life-spans all overlap) were the pioneers who built on Copernicus' beliefs, and created a revolution in scientific thinking which brings the late sixteenth and early seventeenth centuries very close to modern ways of thought. They were Francis Bacon (1561–1626), Galileo (1564–1642), Kepler (1571–1630) and Descartes (1596–1650). It was a revolution which was bearing its first fruits when Christopher Wren was approaching manhood, and it was to this revolution that his life until well after thirty was wholly devoted.

Bacon's contribution was that he phrased in immortal English prose the new approach to the study of all matter, of all thought and of all life. He made no scientific contributions to the New Learning but he was the protagonist of the open mind, the pragmatic approach and the inductive or experimental method.

Galileo's contribution was that by his brilliant experiments he was able to supersede the Aristotelian and Ptolemaic conceptions of the universe, and give Copernicus his rightful place as the first pioneer of modern science. He studied the mechanics of motion and found that all falling bodies fall at the same speed (apart from air-resistance) through distances proportional to the square of the time elapsed. He did not invent the telescope but he improved it vastly, and made excellent use of it. He was the first to observe Jupiter's satellites, the phases of Venus, Saturn's rings, solar spots and lunar mountains, and his study of the pendulum, of the motion of projectiles, and his use of what he called a "thermoscope" (which was in essence the first thermometer, using air and not mercury) were all achievements of the first order. They were, indeed, much too revolutionary for the orthodox ecclesiastics of his day, and he was forced to recant—a process which gave excellent publicity to his revolutionary views.

Kepler was a German astronomer who was an assistant and heir to the aristocratic Copenhagen astronomer Tycho Brahe (1546–1601), and in many ways the precursor of Newton. He was primarily interested in the motions of the planets, and he formulated the three laws of motion which bear his name, and which Newton was to use and acknowledge.

Descartes was both mathematician and philosopher, and his influence on the New Learning was even greater than Bacon's. He was responsible for great improvements in the techniques of algebra, analytical geometry and mechanics, and he was the protagonist of the "dualist" conception which entirely separated soul and body, mind and matter. It was this conception which made it possible to consider the human body as a mere mechanism without running the risk of denying the existence of a soul.

It is to be noted that all these Renaissance pioneers were inventing and using new instruments and new tools. The telescope, though improved by Galileo, had been first developed by a Dutch spectacle-maker in the early 1600s. The microscope was due to two English brothers, Leonard and Thomas Digges, of Queen Elizabeth I's day, and was to be fully exploited by

Wren and his friend and collaborator Robert Hooke. Logarithms were the useful invention of John Napier; the first slide-rule was made by Edward Gunter; and decimal notation was first used by Henry Briggs—all only a few years before the birth of Wren. Galileo's thermometer was followed by his pupil Torricelli's barometer, and the word "electricity" had been coined by Queen Elizabeth's remarkable physician William Gilbert (1540–1603) when his studies in magnetism had led him to discover the curious qualities of amber (ἤλεκτρον). William Harvey (1578–1657), physician to James I, in 1628 had discovered the circulation of the blood, and soon Wren himself was to be verging on the modern techniques of blood transfusion—the traditions of Galen had thus been quickly superseded.

When the seventeen-year-old Christopher Wren was preparing to take up his residence at Wadham College, Oxford, the tragedies of the civil war, which had culminated in the execution of Charles I in January of 1649, were about to be offset by an English renaissance in the fields of science and philosophy which astonished the world. Wren could not have chosen a more exciting period in which to complete his education, and to take his place among those savants and scholars who had been given the Italian name of *virtuosi*—men skilled and learned in their various specialized studies—and who were well equipped to abolish at last the obscurantisms of the Middle Ages and create the bases of all modern scientific progress. Wren was a youthful prodigy fortunate in his heredity, his relatives and his friends.

II

Oxford—1650–56

WHEN WREN BEGAN his university career, Oxford was emerging from the upheavals of the civil war. Academic life had been gravely disturbed, first by the arrival of King, court and royalist army at the beginning of the war, and later from the occupation by the Roundheads after the Cavaliers had retreated westwards. Two years before Wren's arrival, there had been a drastic purge of Oxford's royalist dons, but it was to their credit that the Cromwellians had then "intruded" men of great distinction. They included Dr John Wilkins, Dr Seth Ward, Dr John Wallis, and Dr Lawrence Rooke, all of whom survived to find favour and preferment at the Restoration, and all of whom became the close friends of the young Christopher Wren.

Dr John Wilkins, whom Wren, as we have seen, must already have met in his boyhood when Wilkins was chaplain to the Prince Palatine at Windsor, was a very remarkable man. Aubrey's description of him is far from flattering, and therefore perhaps the more authentic—"he was no great man but one of much and deepe thinking and of a working head, and a prudent man as well as engeniose". He was to marry Cromwell's widowed sister, yet under Charles II he was to be given the bishopric of Chester. The diarist John Evelyn refers to him as "that most obliging and eminently curious Dr Wilkins", and, although that other great diarist, Samuel Pepys, was critical of his preaching, he was delighted with his hospitality and his "most excellent discourse".[1] The Warden of Wadham may not have contributed much in the way of actual inventions to the new scientific Oxford group but he was nevertheless a very vital inspiration and focal point for others. He made his college a rendezvous for all the young savants of his day, and he was sufficiently far-seeing to hold that one day human beings would reach the moon and travel in submarines and flying machines. It is not therefore surprising that, instead of his father's college of St John's, the young Wren had chosen the Wadham of Dr John Wilkins.

At Wadham were Seth Ward and Lawrence Rooke—the one a distinguished astronomer in whose oriel-windowed rooms over the main college gateway Wren found a life-long friendship and later his own lodgings, the other also an astronomer and later a professor of geometry. Wallis from Cambridge was now Oxford's Savilian professor of geometry—he was the mathematician who amongst other things invented the symbol for infinity (∞). Ward, like Wilkins, managed to outlive the odium of the Protectorate—he became Bishop of Salisbury under Charles II. And all these scholars were classed as among "the most celebrated *virtuosi* and Mathematicians of their time"— Wren was honoured in so quickly earning their friendship and esteem.[2]

The usual time taken to achieve the degree of Bachelor of Arts at Oxford was four years. Apparently the statutes were relaxed to permit a precocious Wren to take only two years, and by 1653 at the age of twenty-one he was both a Master of Arts and a Fellow of All Souls.[3] He must have taken the still mediaeval tutelage of the Schools—based on oral disputation and not on written examination—in an easy stride, and at the same time he had found time to stretch his wings in other fields.

In the year of his graduation he had completed "an algebraic tract on the Julian Period" which linked astronomy with universal chronology. He had also invented "a diplographic pen" for writing letters and documents in duplicate which had been brought to the favourable notice of Cromwell, and which was subsequently patented and pirated. In a later letter in which Wren gently complained of this piracy, he finished neatly —"tho I care not for having a Successor in Invention, yet it behoves me to vindicate myself from the Aspersion of having a Predecessor"[4]—Wren was ever of a modest and retiring disposition. And now at All Souls he was able to indulge his zest for research into mathematics, into astronomy, and into every branch of what we now call applied science without the restrictive worry of examinations.

In June of the year 1654, John Evelyn went back to Oxford—
he had been an undergraduate at Balliol—and met for the first
time "that miracle of a youth Mr Christopher Wren". A few
days later, they dined together with Dr John Wilkins "at
Waddum", and there the diarist was shown the Warden's
exhibition of scientific specimens and models to which Wren,
that "prodigious young scholar", had contributed much. It
included "transparent apiaries, a speaking statue, a variety of
shadows, dyals, perspectives, and many other artificial, mathematical and magical curiosities, a way-wiser, a thermometer,
a monstrous magnet, conic and other sections, and a balance
on a demi-circle". The "way-wiser" was an instrument for
automatically registering the distance travelled by a revolving
coach-wheel, and all these fascinating items were in various
ways connected with the geometrical and astronomical experiments which the two friends had been conducting. Wren gave
Evelyn a piece of "white marble which he had stain'd with a
lively red very deepe, as beautiful as if it had been natural"—
an experiment whose purpose is now obscure, but nevertheless
it was an appreciated gesture, and Evelyn became yet another
of Wren's distinguished friends.[5]

One of Wren's early acts on moving to All Souls had been to
design and construct a large and very beautiful sundial for the
south wall of his new college's chapel.[6] It is still to be seen, but
in 1877 it was moved to a similar position on the wall of the
college library. And here, with the aid of his telescope, he
began a study of the planet Saturn which was to occupy him
off and on for many years. Galileo's primitive "tube" had first
observed Saturn's "appendages", but the great pioneer had
been unable to decide upon their form and nature. Wren, with
better instruments, described them as "arms", but his discoveries had been anticipated by the Dutch astronomer Chris-
tiaan Huygens (1629–95) who had decided that they were
"rings", and Wren gallantly confessed that "he loved the invention beyond my own".[7] He had had the help and patronage of
Sir Paul Niele, a rich amateur, and again he had demonstrated
his constructional bent by fashioning models in wax, in pasteboard and in copper to illustrate his theses.

But, while Wren's main interest was still in astronomy, his
lively mind was tempted into other studies—especially into

anatomy and what would now be termed physiology. In *Paren-talia* is a large sheet of elaborate tinted drawings showing the anatomy of the river eel with Latin notes which prove how able Wren was at dissections.[8] In 1656 he initiated and carried through an impressive series of experiments which were to bear precious fruit in modern times. First, he infused liquids directly into the veins of a living dog, and found that he could produce almost any effect he wished. Next, he injected tincture of opium through a quill into the vein of a dog, and produced a stupor which did not kill. Finally, he successfully transfused blood by means of a syringe. Here was a young astronomer casually laying the foundations of the techniques of modern blood transfusions, and also demonstrating the use of what is now called the hypodermic needle.

Dr Wilkins and the great Dr Robert Boyle (1627–91), chemist, physicist and philosopher, were admiring witnesses of these exciting experiments. Wilkins carried them further in experiments of his own eleven years later, but it was not until the comparatively recent discovery of blood groups that the significance of these early Wren experiments was to become fully apparent.[9]

His vivisectional experiments, again carried out with Boyle's help, proved that the spleen could be removed from an animal without endangering life. And it was in Boyle's laboratory that Wren also carried out some valuable experiments which were based on the barometer, which had been invented by Torricelli a dozen years before. They were devised to check the principles enunciated by Descartes, which maintained that the pressure of the moon on the earth's atmosphere, and therefore on the sea, resulted in the phenomena of tides. Wren's work corrected Descartes in several important particulars—for example it proved that variations in the height of the mercury in the barometer bore no relation to the phases of the moon. And from a later Wren letter (1663) we learn that at this time Wren "survey'd a Horse's eye exactly, measuring what the Spheres of the Chrystalline and Cornea were; and what the Proportions of the Distances of the Centres of every Sphere were upon the Axis".[10] He also made an exact model of the human eye—it is significant for his later career that he seemed never to have been satisfied with the abstract unless he was also able to exemplify it by the concrete.

It was in the course of these researches at All Souls that Wren displayed yet another facet of his ability—his draughtsmanship. His beautifully exact drawings of brain dissections done for his friend Dr Thomas Willis (1621–75) were later published and can still be admired.[11] In later years, another friend and collaborator, Robert Hooke, for whom he had done drawings with the aid of a microscope, wrote of Wren in the preface to his *Micrographia* (in which the drawings later appeared) "I must affirm that since the time of Archimedes there scarce ever met in one Man so great a Perfection, such a Mechanical Hand and so philosophical a Mind".[12] And Wren shared with Prince Rupert an enthusiasm for the new "graving in Mezzotinto" which may not have produced masterpieces but which at least brought Wren a welcome annual tribute of wine from the Prince's Rhenish vineyards.[13] There is too a Hollar engraving (1667) of a small landscape view of Windsor Castle which shows Wren's freer hand, and there are the many beautiful architectural drawings of later years to prove his more formal talents. There is the further evidence that Wren's drawings of a louse, a flea and a nit, done with the aid of his magnifying glass, were sufficiently appreciated to be given a place in Charles II's "divine works in the King's closet". Wren's cousin Matthew is an even more enthusiastic witness. When James Harrington baited Oxonians who were "good at two things, at diminishing a Commonwealth and at Multiplying a Louse", Matthew Wren replied that his cousin's drawings were "seen with Delight and Instruction by all Strangers, and not only so but have been received with applause by Foreign Princes".[14] There is therefore no doubt that, while perhaps no great creative artist, Wren had a hand-and-eye ability as a draughtsman of more than average quality.

Of Wren's social life at Oxford there are only occasional glimpses, chiefly through the diaries and letters of his friends. He was fond of amateur theatricals, and took the part of Neanias in a production of Aristophanes' *Plutus* which was acted before his old acquaintance the Prince Palatine in 1651.[15]

He joined in undergraduate journalism by publishing poems in English annexed to an account of how an Oxford servant girl, who had been hanged for murdering her illegitimate child, was revived by medical students to whom the supposed corpse had been sold for dissection.[16] His verse translations of Horace's epistles to Lollius were described by Sprat as "brilliant".

At Oxford, too, he acquired the new and fashionable habit of coffee drinking. The first coffee house in England is reputed to have been opened at The Angel in the parish of St Peter-in-the-East, Oxford, by a Jew named Jacob, and Wood records that in 1655 one Arthur Tillyard ("an apothecary and a great royalist") had opened another coffee house near All Souls, and that Christopher Wren and his two cousins Thomas and Matthew were among its many frequenters.[17] Wren's fondness for his pipe and his coffee in the company of good friends in the coffee house was a habit which was to remain with him all his long life.

There was also a more serious Oxford group—it was almost the equivalent of a modern academic club—of which Wren became a keen member. Its story is revealed in the early pages of Dr Thomas Sprat's *History of the Royal Society*. In about the year 1648, a club devoted to experimental science first met in the Oxford lodgings of Dr William Petty, which were over an apothecary's shop, and therefore conveniently placed for access to any drugs and chemicals which might be required. Later, the club moved to Dr Wilkins' rooms at Wadham, and, when Wilkins left for Trinity, Cambridge, it moved again to Boyle's lodgings in Oxford's High Street, where he had established a small laboratory. Its first purpose, Sprat writes:

was no more than onely the satisfaction of breathing a freer air, and of conversing in quiet one with another without being ingag'd in the passions and madness of that Dismal Age [and] the club was frequented by some *Gentlemen*, of Philosophical Minds whom the misfortunes of the kingdom and the security and ease of a retirement amongst Gown-men, had drawn thither . . . a race of young Men . . . invincibly arm'd against all the inchantments of Enthusiasm.[18]

The times were out of joint, and here was a refuge for thinkers and experimenters who refused to be fanatics in party warfare. Meetings were as frequent as possible, and, rather than debate and discussion, there were "particular Trials in Chymistry or Mechanicks" and a sharing of discoveries.

The principal members were Seth Ward, Wilkins, Wallis, Willis, Rooke, the two Wrens (Christopher and his cousin Matthew), together with Goddard, Bathurst, Petty, Boyle and Hooke. Robert Hooke (1635–1703) had been at Westminster School, and went up to Christ Church, Oxford, in 1653. There he became a chemistry assistant to Willis and later a laboratory assistant to Boyle, who was working on his air pump. He was Wren's junior but already a close friend. Christopher Wren was again fortunate in finding so stimulating a milieu, and the meetings of this "Oxford Group"[19] continued until the death of Cromwell in 1658 and the disturbed period when the Protectorate was in collapse. At that point it became more convenient to resume the meetings in London—and the important sequel to that is a story which will be told later.

A revealing sidelight is thrown on Wren at this period in the story told in *Parentalia* of a meeting with Oliver Cromwell. Probably through Cromwell's brother-in-law Wilkins, Wren had come to know the Claypole family well—Claypole was Cromwell's Master of Horse, and he had married the Protector's favourite daughter. One day, Wren was at dinner with the Claypoles when Cromwell arrived unexpectedly, and in the course of subsequent conversation he turned to the young Wren and said, "Your uncle has long been confined in the Tower." "He has so, sir," replied Wren, "but he bears his Affliction with great Patience and Resignation." "He may come out if he will," was Cromwell's surprising rejoinder. "Will your Highness . . . permit me to tell him this from your own Mouth?" Wren asked. "Yes, you may," said Cromwell; and, as soon as he could, Wren rushed off to tell his uncle the glad news. The stern old royalist was not in the least impressed—"this was not the first Time that he had received the like Intimation from that *Miscreant* but disdained the Terms projected for his Enlargement, which were to be a mean Acknowledgement of his Favour and an abject Submission to his detestable Tyranny."[20] It must have been a disappointment to Christopher, but the old

Bishop did not forget his young nephew—he was to be his first patron in happier times soon to come.

A second revealing episode was concerned with Wren's interest in mathematics. Blaise Pascal (1623–62) was pre-eminently a theologian but he was also interested in mathematics and physics. In 1656 he was in correspondence with the "Oxford Group". He challenged his English friends to solve two problems, one to discover by analysis the point of intersection of a given straight line with an ellipse, and the other to find the dimension and centre of gravity of a body produced by the rotation of a cycloid. He even offered a money prize for correct solutions. Wren sent answers to both questions, but apparently Pascal thought them incomplete, and certainly Wren never received any prize money. On the other hand, he had the pleasure of a genuine compliment from the great French savant—"Il n'y a rien de plus beau que ce qui a été envoyé par Mr Wren," Pascal later recorded.[21]

But perhaps the most impressive evidence of Wren's universality at this early stage of his career is contained in the long list given in *Parentalia* of his chief preoccupations before he left Oxford for London:

> Hypothesis of the moon in solid; to find whether the earth moves; the weather wheel; an artificial eye; to write double by an instrument; a perspective box for surveys; several new ways of graving and etching; to weave many ribbons at once with only turning a wheel; improvements in the arts of husbandry; divers new engines for raising of water; a pavement harder, fairer and cheaper than marble; to grind glasses; a way of embroidery for beds cheap and fair; pneumatic engines; new ways of printing; new designs tending to strength convenience and beauty in building; divers new musical instruments; a speaking organ; new ways of sailing; probable ways for making fresh water at sea; the best way for reckoning time-way-longitude and observing at sea; fabrick for a vessel for war; to build in the sea forts, moles etc.; inventions for better making and fortifying havens, for clearing sands and to sound at sea; to stay long under water; submarine navigation; easier ways of whale-fishing; new cyphers; to pierce a rock in mining; to purge

or vomit or alter the mass by injections into the blood; anatomical experiments; to measure the height of a mountain only by journeying over it; a compass to play in a coach or the hand of a rider; a way of rowing; to perfect coaches for ease, strength and lightness. . . .[22]

The only traces in this formidable list of the Wren known to most people are the references to his interest in building materials, and his desire for new designs for strength, convenience and beauty in building. For the rest it is an impressively varied catalogue of the activities of an all-embracing brain whose only superior would be that of a Leonardo da Vinci.

III

Gresham and The Royal Society—1657-61

WREN'S FIRST PUBLIC appointment came at the early age of 25—in 1657 he was offered the chair of astronomy at Gresham College in the City of London. He accepted it.

Gresham College had been first endowed some 60 years before by Sir Thomas Gresham, the Elizabethan founder of the Royal Exchange and England's first great merchant-banker. He had bequeathed his large house and enclosed garden (which lay between modern Bishopsgate and Broad Street) jointly to the City of London and the Mercers' Company. It provided living quarters, lecture rooms, a laboratory and an observatory for seven unmarried professors each of whom enjoyed an honorarium of £50 a year, and whose sole duty was to give public lectures—as there were no resident students there were no burdensome tutorial duties. There were seven weekly lectures—on divinity, astronomy, geometry, music, law, physic and rhetoric, and, as in Wren's day the chairs of music and rhetoric were both tenanted by scientists, in effect the whole college had become a small university for the popularization and encouragement of the new approach to scientific problems in all fields.

Wren's own chair had just been vacated by his old Wadham colleague Lawrence Rooke—he had transferred to the chair of geometry—and the other professors were also his friends. Each professor was obliged to give one weekly lecture on his own subject, in the morning in Latin and after the midday dinner in English, and the audiences were largely composed of City fathers. It was a remarkable early experiment in what would in modern times be called adult education, and it was also a far-seeing endowment of academic scholarship and practical research.[1]

Wren's Gresham lectures—chiefly on the astronomy of
Kepler—have unfortunately not survived, but both the Latin
and English versions of his inaugural address can still be read—
they are interesting documents. The young professor outlined
the new-fashioned attitude to his very ancient subject—
astronomy. Instead of the mediaeval approach through Aristotelian logic, he preferred the new routes through mathematics,
as recommended by Francis Bacon and exemplified by Descartes. He was sufficiently aware of his special audience to refer
to the needs of navigation, and he assured them that God
Almighty was still "the finest and greatest of the geometers".
But he also gave them a more heterodox explanation of the
biblical story of the Holy Sepulchre which illustrates his sense
of humour. Jesus could only be said to have been three days and
three nights in the tomb if the chronicler were taking account
of the fact that, while the hemisphere of Jordan was experi-
encing a day and two nights, the other hemisphere was experi-
encing a night and two days—a total of three days and three
nights in respect of the earth considered as a whole! There is
also one very startling note which comes ringing down the
corridors of time to strike a familiar chord for our own day—
"future ages may find the Galaxy (of stars) to be myriads of
them, and every nebulous star appearing as if it were the Firma-
ment of some other World—hang'd in the vast abyss of inter-
mundious vacuum". And he sums up the whole Baconian
movement of his period in the famous passage which reads
"Mathematical Demonstrations built upon the impregnable
foundations of Geometry and Arithmetick are the only Truths
that can sink into the Mind of Man void of all Uncertainty, and
all other Discourses participate more or less of Truth according
as Their Subjects are more or less capable of Mathematical
Demonstration."

His practical approach was illustrated by his plan for the
compilation of a complete meteorological record which would
relate weather to epidemics—a suggestion which he was to
repeat later before the Royal Society. His enthusiasm for the
work of Galileo and Kepler and their "elliptical" astronomy
and his interest in new theories of "dioptrics"—in "refraction"
—were expressed in equally practical plans for improvements
in the special instruments of his profession—telescopes and

lenses. In both versions, Wren's Inaugural illustrates his sensibility and his practicality—he was never an ivory-tower philosopher—and they prove equally his wide scholarship and his shrewd wit.[2]

Wren's stay at Gresham was not of long duration, but it was long enough for him to demonstrate there his hypotheses of Saturn's "rings", and to place in the college courtyard a copper model of his theories on an obelisk paid for by his wealthy friend and patron Sir Paul Niele, who had also in the spring of 1658 obligingly erected a new telescope for him.

In the following September, Oliver Cromwell died. It was the end of an era, and for a time there was a serious possibility of anarchy. The Protector's son was a poor substitute for his father, and the Roundhead army took over the government of the whole country. Gresham College became a cavalry barracks, and the only professor who was allowed to continue in residence was Dr Goddard, the professor of physic who had been Oliver Cromwell's personal doctor. As an educational institution, Gresham was out of action for over a year, and Wren retired to the shelter of All Souls at Oxford. When Gresham was at last evacuated, Dr Sprat wrote to Wren that he had found the college "in such a nasty condition, so defiled and the smells so infernal that, if you should now come to make use of your tube, it would be like Dives looking out of Hell into heaven".[3] Meanwhile, we know from Wood that, on Boyle's suggestion, Wren attended lectures given in Oxford in 1659 by the noted chemist and Rosicrucian "Peter Sthael of Strasburg in Royal Prussia— a Lutheran, a great hater of women and a very useful man".[4]

But what had happened to the "experimental philosophical Clubbe" which had first begun to meet at Oxford ten years before? For various reasons the academic friends who had first composed it had been scattered, but the majority had contrived to meet again in London, usually at Gresham College after the Wednesday and Thursday lectures of Wren and Rooke. In 1658 they had again been separated "by the miserable distractions of that fatal year", but early in 1659 work was resumed at Gresham (Wren was lecturing there on light and refraction) and the "Clubbe" revived.

On 29 May 1660, Charles II re-entered London as king— it was his birthday, and Evelyn has left a lively description of the tumultous welcome he received from the citizens. It was a happy time, too, for Wren. His famous uncle was promptly released from the Tower, and restored in triumph to his bishopric of Ely. His cousin Matthew—a fellow *virtuoso*—was appointed secretary to the new Lord Chancellor, Edward Hyde, soon to be made Earl of Clarendon. And once again the Wren family were close to court circles.

Wren's first responsibility was to carry out the duty imposed upon him by his late father—he had died at Bletchingdon two years before the Restoration for which he had hoped so long. Wren handed over to the new Dean of Windsor the Garter record books which his father had saved from destruction during the civil war. And on 28 November of this same happy Restoration year, after one of Wren's Gresham lectures, he and a dozen old friends withdrew to Rooke's quarters and there took the first steps towards formally constituting a new society —"a designe of founding a College for the promotion of Physico-Mathematicall Experimental learning".[5] It was to meet regularly on Wednesdays at three in the afternoon either at Rooke's chambers in Gresham or Bolles' in the Temple. On 5 December, Sir Robert Moray, who was one of the group, and now the King's chief advisor on Scottish affairs, brought the good news that the King himself was interested in the project, and was even prepared to grant it a royal charter. Those present forthwith signed a document—it is still at the Royal Society—binding them "to consult and debate concerning the promotion of Experimental learning", and that "each will allowe one shilling weekly towards the defraying of occasional charges".[6] What was soon to become the Royal Society was thus safely launched. It was John Evelyn who gave it its famous name. On 3 December 1661, he wrote in his diary:

by universal suffrage of our Philosophic Assembly, an order was made & registered that I should receive their Publique Thanks for the honourable mention I made of them by the name of *Royal Society*, in my Epistle Dedicatory to the Lord Chancellor, before my Traduction of Naudens. Too greate an honour for a trifel.[7]

In all these proceedings, Christopher Wren had been an enthusiastic protagonist. He was now asked to draw up a suggested preamble for the proposed royal charter, and *Parentalia* prints his rough draft. Naturally, it is a somewhat florid piece of prose, but behind the resounding rhetoric appropriate to a royal proclamation there is a typical insistence upon the social usefulness of the new experimental science.[8] In September 1661, the new society obtained its first royal warrant, and on 15 July 1662 it received its final royal charter—the official date for the founding of the Royal Society.

It was not the earliest scientific society of the seventeenth century, but it rapidly became the most influential. As early as 1560, there had been an Academia Secretorum Naturae at Naples; from 1603 to 1630, an Accademia dei Lincei worked in Rome; and in 1651, the Accademia del Cimento had been founded by the Medicis in Florence. But the Royal Society had forestalled Louis XIV's Académie des Sciences by some four years, and its rules were infinitely more progressive. It was to be open to men of any religious faith, of any nationality, of any profession and of any trade, although it was deemed inevitable that its first members would be English "gentlemen free and unconfin'd", or, in other words, with the means and leisure to be able to help in the Society's chosen work. It was a self-elected society of academics, scholars and "amateurs", who had created their own assembly and who controlled their own future—it was not the creation of government or monarchy. The Society made gallant efforts to reform the contemporary complexity of academic language, preferring the language of the people; and, in Sprat's noble phrase, its ultimate aim was to make itself "the general *Banck* and Free-port of the World". It was not the least of Christopher Wren's contributions to the best interests of science that he pioneered the origins, became one of the founder members, and never lost interest in the welfare of the Royal Society.[9]

Between 1661 and 1663, Wren seems to have divided his time between All Souls at Oxford and visits to London for meetings of the new society. In May of 1661 his friend Seth Ward was appointed Bishop of Exeter, and therefore had to resign his

Savilian professorship of astronomy at Oxford. Wren was elected
in his place, and in the same year his academic career was
crowned by the honour of DCL degrees at both Oxford and
Cambridge. He lectured on spheres, on Pascal, and on navigation at All Souls, and in the pages of Balthasar de Monconys'
Voyages d'Angleterre (1663) there is an intriguing sidelight on
Wren as the supreme Oxford *virtuoso* of his day—

> Besides the College which I went to see, as I did all the others
> out of curiosity, I went there [i.e. to All Souls] even more to
> see Mr Renes the great Mathematician, though a slight man,
> but at the same time one of the most civil and frank that I
> have met in England; for though he was unwilling that his
> ideas should be made publicke he did not hesitate to tell me
> most freely of . . .

and there follows an impressive list of his scientific activities.[10]

But soon the claims on Wren of the Society in London became
paramount. He was asked to prepare experiments on the pendulum and on solar eclipses, and he was kept busy on a committee of the society which was studying the production of lenses.
His work came to the notice of the King, and he was commanded to produce a series of microscopical drawings of insects,
and to supply a large-scale globe model of the moon "representing not only the spots and various degrees of whiteness upon the
surface, but the hills, eminences and cavities moulded in solid
work" for the King's private museum. He was able to excuse
himself from the first task, but he completed the second. His
model could be turned to the light to reveal all the monthly
phases of the moon "with the variety of appearances that
happen from the shadows of the mountains and valleys". It
must have been a very impressive construction, and it was set
up on a turned stand of *lignum vitae* with a scale and a loyal
inscription worthy of it.[11]

On 20 May 1662, Charles II was married to the Portuguese
princess, Catherine of Braganza, and her dowry included the
Moroccan port of Tangier. It was decided that efforts should be
made to convert Tangier into a useful naval base, and a royal

commissioner was needed "to survey and direct the works of the mole, harbour and fortifications of the citadel and town". The post was offered to Christopher Wren.

That a Savilian professor of astronomy should have been offered such a position is at first sight surprising. But in the seventeenth century there were no separate professions of architecture and engineering. There were skilled craftsmen, artificers, stonemasons, carpenters and builders of all kinds, but there were no professional controllers of such activities with authoritative qualifications and training. The most desirable equipment of such controllers would have been a knowledge of the mathematical sciences, including especially what are now termed mechanics and geometry, and an ability to design and to illustrate designs on paper. Seen with these requirements in mind, Wren was by no means an outsider—after all, he was "esteemed one of the best geometers in Europe", and his wide range of studies and inventions covered such apposite matters as the best methods of constructing moles and fortifying havens. It was a very tempting offer—the position carried with it an ample salary, a temporary dispensation from his professorial duties, and, much more important, it was indicated to Wren that the very impressive office of Surveyor-General of the Royal Works would be at his disposal on the death of its then occupant. It must have been a surprise to all his friends that Wren politely excused himself on health grounds, and he seems to have managed his refusal with considerable adroitness—the King was in no way offended.[12]

It was perhaps more than a mere coincidence that at the time of so flattering a sign of royal favour Wren was embarking on yet another activity as an amateur which was eventually to result in his holding as a professional the surveyorship which at this stage he seems to have so lightly turned down. Between the year 1662 and the year 1669, when Christopher Wren became in effect chief architect to the crown of England, the scientist and astronomer was slowly metamorphosed into the architect. But before that fascinating process is described in detail, some attempt must be made to sum up and assess the worth of his first career as scientist.

As astronomer—and that was his official position for twelve years—Wren's contribution was first to improve the tools of his profession. He refined the mechanics of the "tubes" of his day —he himself owned a telescope of 36 feet in length, and co-operated with Wilkins in constructing one of 80 feet for studying the moon—and he perfected ingenious machines for the grinding of lenses of all shapes and sizes. Second, he used his improved instruments to study the rings of Saturn and the moons of Jupiter, and add to our knowledge of the moon. But perhaps his most original contribution to astronomy was his scheme for a graphical construction to explain and compute solar and lunar eclipses and occultations of the stars. It is typical of Wren that this particular activity, although approved by Flamsteed, the first Astronomer Royal, was not published until 1681, and then in the work of another mathematician. Wren's methods have been used ever since, and they were suitably acknowledged in a modern Gresham astronomer's essay in the Wren bi-centenary volume compiled by the RIBA in 1923.[13] Wren's work on comets was similarly revealed later. His friend Robert Hooke did much work on a comet which appeared at the end of the year 1664, and, in his posthumous works published in 1678, he maintains that Wren's methods for predicting comets and their paths were unsurpassed though hitherto unacknowledged— they were actually presented to the Royal Society in 1665.[14]

As a meteorologist Wren again contributed first an improvement in instruments—his weather clock with its various components for the automatic measuring and registration of rainfall, humidity, temperature, pressure and wind has already been mentioned. Wren himself never perfected it, but in 1679 Hooke presented a finished version to the Royal Society. Wren's second meteorological contribution is perhaps more impressive —in an address to the Royal Society on 9 December 1663 he detailed his programme for a comprehensive diary of the seasons in all their meteorological phases, which, if it had been carried out, would have anticipated the work of the Meteorological Office by over a century.[15]

As a pure mathematician, Wren had contemporary rivals, but no superior. He had been able to match his wits with those of Pascal, and in 1658 he could claim that he had discovered the rectification of the cycloid—a straight line of equivalent length to the curve described by a point in the circumference of a rolling circle. He wrote four tracts on this abstruse subject and in 1658 handed them over to his friend Dr John Wallis, who later published them.[16]

As what in modern terms would be called a physicist, Wren perhaps made his greatest contribution to the history of science. He had been fascinated with the earlier experiments of Descartes, who, using billiard balls and tennis balls, had first approached satisfactory laws of motion, and in 1662 he himself constructed an experiment with suspended balls to help to determine finally the laws of impact. In 1668 Wren, Wallis and Huygens were invited by the Royal Society to take these experiments further.

Meanwhile, a younger Cambridge scholar—one Isaac Newton (1642-1727)—had been elaborating his famous theory of gravitation and its laws. In 1687, Newton's *Principia* burst on the scientific scene, and early in that monumental work Newton went out of his way to pay unqualified tribute to Wren and his colleagues—Dr Wallis and Mr Huygens—

> the greatest geometers of our times, did severally determine the rules of the collision and mutual rebound of hard bodies, and much about the same time communicated their discoveries to the Royal Society, exactly agreeing among themselves as to those rules. Dr Wallis, indeed, was something more early in the publications, then followed Sir Christopher Wren, and lastly Mr Huygens. But Sir Christopher Wren confirmed the truth of the theory before the Royal Society by the experiment of suspended balls.[17]

Yet there have been critics who have accused Wren of being a mere scientific gadget-maker! Wren, it is true, could take pleasure in devising such minor conveniences as a long-lived lamp, warm box-beehives, a duplicating pen, a coach compass, a "way-wiser", a perspective-box, a bowl-level using mercury, and better hot-houses, and he could exercise his ingenuity on the humdrum problems of raising weights, the force of gunpowder, better ways of swimming, rowing and sailing, and blacklead as a lubricant for clocks; but he was capable too of the broader vision and the longer view.[18] Wren's reputation as a scientist can safely rest on the laurels which Newton was ready so generously to bestow.

IV

Astronomer into Architect—1662–6

———————————

SEVEN YEARS SEPARATED Wren's refusal to go to Tangier
from his acceptance of the post of Surveyor-General of the
Royal Works in 1669—they were in a sense the traditional
seven years of an apprenticeship to architecture. Throughout,
he retained his Savilian chair of astronomy at Oxford—in fact
he did not resign it until 1673—but he was increasingly involved in the arts and crafts of building until at last in his
mid-thirties it became clear as to where his future destiny lay.
It is necessary, therefore, to review the state of architecture as
Wren saw it, and to appreciate the work of his immediate predecessors and contemporaries, if his future career is to be
correctly assessed.

In England, it was not until the early nineteenth century
that an organized profession of architecture finally emerged.
Before that, an architect was, as the derivation of the word
indicates, a chief-builder, and there was a native tradition of
master-building and its associated skills which derived from the
Middle Ages. The mediaeval cathedrals and monastic houses
were the products of community craftsmanship, although from
time to time such leading artificers as the great Henry Yevele
of Chaucer's day had become something more.[1] The Royal
Office of Works was a part of the English royal household, and
it gradually became a nursery of master-craftsmen of all kinds;
in the sixteenth century its Surveyor-General became the
crown's chief architect responsible for the planning, erection
and maintenance of all royal properties.[2] But the valuable
post of Surveyor-General might be given to a court favourite
or to a distinguished administrator from other fields, and the
royal buildings frequently benefited from the inspirations of
gifted amateurs. In Italy, where the traditions of Gothic archi-

tecture had least hold, and where in the early fifteenth century the new architecture first flourished, the architect of the great cathedral at Florence was Brunelleschi—a goldsmith; its bell-tower was the design of Giotto—a painter; at Rome the new St Peter's owed much to Michelangelo and Bernini—both primarily sculptors; and in France Louis XIV entrusted the new east front of his Louvre palace to Claude Perrault—originally a physician. When Charles II offered the surveyor-generalship to an astronomer he was not entirely out of fashion.

But what had the Middle Ages bequeathed to anyone inter-ested in the arts and crafts of building in early seventeenth-century England? There were about 30 magnificent Gothic cathedrals, the impressive remains of over 600 monastic abbeys, as many as 14,000 parish churches most of which had some feature of merit, about 500 castles in varying stages of pictur-esque disrepair, and seven greater lay-buildings which deserved the name of royal palaces. In domestic architecture there was a less impressive legacy, but there were hundreds of stone manor houses in which the "hall" was still the major room and not yet merely the lobby, most towns had excellent examples of mediaeval half-timbered citizen's houses, and sometimes alms-houses and schools, and at the two universities and the Inns of Court there were traditions of sound design and construction which applied the arts and crafts of church and hall to the needs of academic community living.

It was in early Tudor times that these placid but dis-tinguished mediaeval traditions had been first disturbed by the revolutionary movement which is termed the Renaissance. England was introduced to the heady influence of classical antiquities, and to new enthusiasms—stemming from Italy and from France—for an architecture based on the achievements of ancient Rome.

The chief agency which speeded the new architectural gospel was the printing press. Throughout the sixteenth century, editions of books on classical architecture were hurried from the new machines and distributed throughout Europe. The earliest known treatise on Roman architecture was the work of Vitruvius, who had compiled it in the time of the Emperor Augustus. It was first printed in 1486, and in 1556 a superb Italian version was printed in Venice illustrated by Palladio.

The first contemporary work on architecture to be printed, *De Re Aedificatoria*, was published in 1485 by Alberti, who was both a student of ancient Roman architecture and a designer in the new mode. He was followed by Vignola of Bologna, whose *Five Orders of Architecture* (1562) had wide influence in France, and by Serlio whose *Architettura* was probably the most popular architectural treatise of the Renaissance in all countries.

Palladio (1508–80), however, by what he built even more than by what he wrote, was the most widely respected of all the Italian Renaissance masters. He was born at Padua and spent most of his working life as a mason at Vicenza. He was later able to travel and to study at Rome, and his famous *Four Books on Architecture* were first published in Venice in 1570 and many times reprinted and translated. His most celebrated masterpieces are the church of San Giorgio Maggiore at Venice and the Villa Capra (or Rotonda) at Vicenza, and his greatest English admirer was Inigo Jones. The most influential architectural book of English origin was the *First and Chief Groundes of Architecture* published by John Shute in 1563, and at the same period there were many books available from Paris and Antwerp illustrating the French and Flemish versions of the new style. And copies of all the best available works on architecture were later to be found in the personal library of Sir Christopher Wren.

What were the essentials of this new style? A revival of the semi-circular arch as the perfect support for wall, floor or roof; a revival of the Roman stone pillars designed in the approved five "orders" (adapted from Etruscan and Grecian origins) for carrying arches or architraves in temples and amphitheatres, or adapted as pilasters to great walls; a revived delight in such classical ornamentation as swags, shields, wreaths, urns, weaponry, armour and portrait busts translated into stone and marble with consummate skill; and finally a passion for the "cupola" or dome, which classical Rome had borrowed from the Near East. It was a new style based on past standards and disciplines, but it was a style which also permitted an infinite variety of treatment, and was about to give the widening civilized world ecclesiastical, civic and domestic architectural masterpieces.

And the new Renaissance mode was superbly relevant to

the new needs of both the Protestant and the Romanist versions of the Christian religion. The reformed Church now needed great preaching halls—the worship of the saints in secluded side-chapels was banned, and procession-paths were no longer essential. In the Romanist church, too, there was a call for mass meeting places as well as preaching auditoria—the clergy was no longer a separate race of mankind needing exclusive and secluded areas for corporate ceremonials and private devotions. A mediaeval Gothic cathedral such as Salisbury could only be adapted to the new reformed religion with great difficulty and much waste of space. When the Romanists needed a new St Peter's, they found ready to hand a new architectural style tailored to the new outlook of people and clergy, and as the Jesuits flourished to lead a counter-Reformation they too found the new style ideal for the vast preaching assembly halls they required. Renaissance architecture was not just a harking-back revivalism, it was keyed to the essential needs of contemporary living.

In England, it was the royal patronage of skilled immigrants and distinguished visitors which first inspired actual examples of the new fashion. Torrigiano from Italy gave Henry VIII the superb un-Gothic tomb (1512-19) for his father. Other Italian craftsmen gave a classical flavour to Wolsey's Hampton Court (1531), and enabled his master to endow Cambridge with the superb Renaissance screen and stalls of King's College Chapel (1533-50), and to build for himself the fantastic and rightly named Nonsuch Palace which brought a caricatured Loire château to the banks of the Thames (1538).[3] Under Queen Elizabeth I—she was never a spender—the great builders were the new aristocrats, who had founded family and fortunes on the ecclesiastical confiscations of the Reformation and the new wealth deriving from a wider world. There was Sir Thomas Gresham's new Royal Exchange, and the astonishing crafts-manship of the roof and screen of the Middle Temple's hall. Towards the end of her reign there came such great "Jacobe-than" houses as Longleat (1572-7), Burghley (1575-7) and Theobalds (1574). Under James I, it was the Netherlanders' turn to influence English buildings. We know that Audley End (1603-16) was built by the Dutch Bernard Jaansen; and Hat-field (1607-11), Bramshill (1601-12), Charlton House, Green-

wich (1607) and Holland House (1606–7) are all witnesses to
the Dutch vogue. Under Charles I there was Sir Balthazar
Gerbier's pretty York Water Gate (1626) built for the Duke of
Buckingham, the gifted amateur Sir Roger Townshend's Rayn-
ham Hall (1635) in Norfolk, and the London craftsmen who
built the Dutch House (1631) at Kew, Swakeleys (1638) in
Middlesex, Cromwell House (1637–8) in Highgate and Lindsey
House (1640) in Lincoln's Inn Fields. And it was under the
first two Stuarts that one of our greatest architects, in the
modern sense, flourished in the person of their Surveyor-General
—Inigo Jones.

Inigo Jones (1573–1652) held the office of Surveyor-General
of the Royal Works until the outbreak of the civil war in 1642.[4]
The son of a London cloth worker, he made his own way in
contemporary arts by virtue of his skill as a draughtsman and
his flair for devising and producing the then fashionable court
masques. He had travelled to Denmark and Italy, and in 1611
he had found a cultured patron in the heir to the English
throne—Prince Henry. Unfortunately, in the following year
this brilliant young prince died of typhoid fever, and Inigo
Jones set off on his travels again. This time he went to Venice
and to Rome, where he was able to make a concentrated study
of Roman antiquities, and to check by his own careful measure-
ments the work in print and stone of such later masters as
Palladio. On his way home, he was also able to view such
famous ancient provincial Roman monuments as the Maison
Carrée at Nîmes, and some of the new French châteaux in the
Loire country. By the time he took over the surveyorship he
was indeed an architect, if not academically qualified by
apprenticeship and examination, yet superbly equipped by
genius and experience. He was able to hand on to Wren's day
some Renaissance masterpieces which have never been
surpassed.

His Queen's House at Greenwich was begun for James I's
Queen, Anne of Denmark, and completed for Henrietta Maria,
Queen of Charles I. It is still in pride of place as the focal point
of the great Greenwich Hospital complex, to which Wren was
to contribute so much. Jones' perfect Banqueting House (with
its Rubens ceiling) for a new Whitehall Palace still stands
superbly superior to its sham-renaissance civil-service neigh-

bours. His Queen's Chapel at St James's Palace was the earliest ecclesiastical building in England in what Wren called the new "Roman manner", and it still retains its dignity and quiet charm. Of his laying-out of a square and piazza at Covent Garden and its new parish church of St Paul, which was its centre piece, only a few drawings and the much-altered church itself remain, but there is still sufficient evidence to rank Inigo Jones as one of our earliest and most distinguished town planners.

Of his major work at mediaeval Old Paul's there is only the evidence of engravings, and the printed admiration of Wren himself. It was a bold and even a revolutionary conception. The mediaeval cathedral had been allowed to fall into a deplorable state of disrepair. Its tower was a mere stump of its former 500 feet of glory, its fourteenth-century Gothic east end was capable of reasonable repair but its Romanesque nave needed more drastic treatment. Jones daringly cased-in the Norman nave with new Renaissance masonry, added transept doors, and at the west end built a new portico of classical Corinthian columns flanked by Renaissance towers and surmounted by a pediment in a style which had direct links with ancient Rome and the architecture of such a Roman revivalist as Palladio. There is no doubt that it was a breath-taking achievement, and, if some contemporaries were shocked, Inigo Jones' contribution to Old Paul's was to earn the unqualified approval of Christopher Wren—he described it as "an entire and excellent piece".

After the civil war began, in 1642, there was of course very little building of note in England for nearly twenty years. But, with the restoration of Charles II in 1660, the office of the Royal Works was promptly revived by a monarch with a lively, if somewhat cynical,[5] interest in all contemporary arts and sciences, and an ambition to rival the artistic achievements of Louis XIV across the Channel. By this time Inigo Jones was dead—he had fought for the King and died in obscurity in 1652. His successor—if merit and experience had been the criteria—should have been his chief assistant John Webb.

Webb had built at least two distinguished great houses—at

Gunnersbury in Middlesex and at Amesbury in Wiltshire (both
of which have gone) but he contributed the King Charles block
to the new palace at Greenwich which still survives in all its
severe and admirable grandeur. Both Charles II and history
treated John Webb shamefully; but the returning monarch
had to reward those who had supported him in exile, and he
appointed Sir John Denham to be his new Surveyor-General.
Denham was a minor poet and had little or no interest in
architecture—but he had been a loyal Cavalier. However, his
Paymaster at the Royal Works was indeed an architect—Hugh
May.[6] He, like Denham, had spent much of the civil-war period
in exile in Holland, and he had brought back with him to
England the new Dutch version of the Renaissance style exemplified in the beautiful Mauritshuis of Van Campen at The
Hague. May's architecture displayed a very acceptable combination of brick with classical stone pilasters which was
admirably suited to the new country houses which the returning
aristocrats required, and his Eltham Lodge has been the model
for many subsequent elegant mansions in the new manner,
some of which have been frequently and wrongly attributed
to Wren.

Contemporary with May was the very able amateur Roger
Pratt. He had avoided the civil war, as his friend John Evelyn
had done, by travelling abroad to France, Holland and Italy.
He had returned to England after the execution of Charles I,
and had managed to keep himself out of political trouble. He
built five large mansions, and two of them—Coleshill in Berk-
shire and Clarendon House in Piccadilly—were of prophetic
consequence. Nothing of his work now survives but there are
photographs of Coleshill—it was burned down as recently as
1962—and there is an excellent engraving of Clarendon House,
which Evelyn described as "without hyperbolies the best contriv'd, the most usefull, gracefull and magnificent house in
England". It was the Stuart great house *par excellence*, and it was
the inspiration for many successors of lesser quality but similar
provenance. Pratt's life as an amateur architect was short but
fruitful, and it was a loss to English architecture that he retired
so early to become a knighted country squire in his native
Norfolk.[7]

Christopher Wren was very much the child of his period. He must have been well aware of the architectural heritage of his native land, and, as an Oxonian he cannot have been blind to the Renaissance Canterbury quadrangle of St John's College, which had been started just before he was born, and the extravagant but exciting Renaissance porch of St Mary the Virgin, built when he was a schoolboy. And then, just after he had turned down the Tangier appointment, he received the invitation which was to change his life.

Gilbert Sheldon, Bishop of London, had been ejected from his wardenship of All Souls in 1648 by the Puritans, but shortly before the Restoration he had been reinstated. He knew Wren well. As bishop he was responsible for the welfare of Old Paul's, and, in spite of Inigo Jones' improvements and additions, its fabric had suffered grievously from the vandalism of the Cromwellian army—its nave had even stabled cavalry. Sheldon turned to Wren for help and advice.

It is not clear precisely when Wren was first consulted, but it could have been as early as 1661. Meanwhile, Sheldon also honoured his old friend with a private commission. Sheldon was a rich man and a grateful Oxonian. He had seen too much of the hooliganism which was the usual accompaniment to the annual conferment of university degrees—known as "The Act" —which took place in the university church of St Mary's in the High Street. He had decided to symbolize his love of Oxford by the gift of a special lay building in which "The Act" could be performed without offence to sanctity, and he asked Wren to design it for him. The result was what is known as the Sheldonian Theatre. In April 1663, Wren showed a model of his proposed design to his colleagues of the Royal Society, the foundation stone was laid in the following year, and the completed building was opened with great ceremony six years later. It is still in use for the purpose for which it was designed.

The Sheldonian, as it is familiarly called, has always had its critics, and it is interesting especially because it illustrates both the limitations and the genius of its learner-designer. Considering its avowed purpose, Wren unhesitatingly decided that fundamentally it must be a theatre, and as a true disciple of the new architectural faith he went straight to ancient Rome for inspiration. In Serlio he found engravings and descriptions of the Theatre of Marcellus—its ruins still survive—which was an open-air theatre protected from the elements only by awnings. Wren had to adapt the Roman plan to the available site, solve the problems of roofing-in an area of some 80 by 70 feet without impeding pillars, and decide upon the lighting and the décor— it was both an exercise in engineering and a question of aesthetics.

Fortunately, Wren's friend and colleague, Dr John Wallis, then Savilian professor of geometry at Oxford, had already experimented with timbers jointed to bridge a span considerably longer than the length of the separate pieces of timber. His research had begun at Cambridge in 1644, and had resulted at the Restoration in models of his ingenious "geometrical flat floor", which had found an honoured place in Charles II's private museum, winning the approval of the Royal Society. Wren adapted the same principles to his theatre roof, using what engineers call the "vertical truss" construction—his skill as a "geometer" was already serving him well in his new career.[8] The Sheldonian's roof astonished and delighted contemporary virtuosi. Fifty years later, after its ceiling had been carrying the additional weight of the bookstore of the university press, it was suspected of weakening, but a skilled inspection pronounced it good for "one hundred or two hundred years to come", and, although needing renovation in the nineteenth century, it still survives.

The treatment of the ceiling under the trusses illustrates Wren's discreet sense of humour. He persuaded the painter Robert Streeter to decorate it with a trompe l'oeil design which depicted the open sky of Italy with a classical "velarium" held back by golden cords to permit the descent of allegorical figures portraying the triumph of Learning and Justice over Envy and Malice.[9] Beneath the floor, there was accommodation for the university printing-presses, and, in the centre of the south front, great doors provided for the university's ceremonial processions. The northern half of the building is contained in a semi-circle, and its interior carries a shallow gallery for more spectators; it is well lit by ample clear-glass windows, and provided with wooden stalls and carving of excellent quality.

It is the Sheldonian's exterior which has caused so much controversy. The straight south front is a somewhat elementary exercise in the use of Corinthian pilasters and half-columns under a double pediment which bears no relation to the rest of the curved exterior with its uninspired windows, its rusticated arched walling and its inconsequential swaggings. The outside roof, however, as Wren designed it, was more original—its charming oval dormer windows radiated from a graceful central turret, but in 1838 these dormers were removed and the turret altered, and today's Sheldonian is less satisfying than it was.

Some architectural pundits have not been slow to condemn its whole conception, and at the Wren Commemoration Banquet in 1923 the then President of the RIBA pronounced it "a shapeless lump" and "the worst building erected in Oxford prior to the Gothic revival".[10] But there is no doubt that to generations of Oxford men (and lately women) this first Wren building has always been regarded with great affection.

It may be that its surrounding railings, which are strengthened by fourteen stone piers each surmounted by a grotesque bust, which the poor quality of the stone and the weathering of time quickly made even more grotesque, and which have always tempted the ribaldry of successive generations of undergraduates, was a deliberate practical joke in stone. Wren's undergraduate days were not so very far away, and he must have frequently witnessed the traditional rowdyism of "The Act". The busts (are they caesars or ancient philosophers?) have recently once again been restored, and they may owe their original existence to the grille of similar pattern at the château of Vaux le Vicomte near Paris, which Wren visited on his only journey abroad. The critics who condemn the architecture of the Sheldonian Theatre might with more justice have condemned its protective railings; for the most part they have ignored them. Today, the Sheldonian—with all its faults and its many ingenuities—is still an example of one definition of good design: it is admirably fitted for its purpose.

While the Sheldonian was being built, Wren undertook another but lesser private commission.[11] His uncle—the persecuted and redoubtable Matthew Wren, Bishop of Ely—wished to present his old college of Pembroke, Cambridge, with a new chapel in fulfilment of a vow made when he was in the Tower, and he asked his nephew to design it. The result was the first college chapel in England built in the new style. It is a very simple and very dignified oblong design which uses semi-circular windows and niches and Corinthian pilasters to support a wide-eaved pedimented roof surmounted by a hexagonal bell turret, and its interior is equally dignified and classical.

Pembroke chapel was begun in 1663 and completed by 1665, by which date Christopher Wren had decided that a visit to France, where there was a veritable spate of new building, would be of the greatest service to him. On 22 June 1665, he was writing to his old friend and Royal Society colleague Dr Bathurst, then President of Trinity College, Oxford, concerning some projected new buildings for the college, and he mentions that within a fortnight he hoped to be in Paris and meeting "Mons. Mansart and Signor Bernini".[12] He had obtained an introduction to the Earl of St Albans, who was Charles II's representative at St Germain, and he had provided himself with introductions also to the many architects then working in or near the French capital, where he spent eight or nine busy months from July 1665 to March 1666. One long letter from Wren, and two mentions in shorter letters from friends, enable a reasonably accurate description of the visit to be made.

Although he found time to meet some of the French mathematicians, his main concern was to see as much as he could of the new French architecture, and to meet some of the fashionable French and Italian architects then in Paris.[13] He spent much time at the new Louvre palace, studying not only its architecture but more especially the engineering which made its construction possible—he described it as "a School of Architecture the best probably at this Day in Europe", and was very impressed with the efficiency of Colbert, the King's *Surveillant des Bâtiments*. In the company of the son of Sir Thomas Browne —the great literary doctor of Norwich—he made a tour of mansions near Paris including le Raincy, whose domed saloon by Louis le Vau greatly pleased him. He twice visited Versailles, then but a brick and stone hunting lodge too lavishly decorated for Wren's masculine taste:

not an inch within but is crowded with little Curiosities of
Ornaments: the Women, as they make here the language
and Fashion, and meddle with Politicks and Philosophy, so
they sway also in Architecture; Works of Filgrand and little
Knacks are in great Vogue, but Building certainly ought to
have the Attribute of eternal and therefore the only Thing
uncapable of new Fashions.

He saw the King's châteaux at Fontainebleau and St Ger-
main and the Palais Mazarin, and many times admired the
Queen Mother's apartments in the Louvre. He visited the
great mansions of Vaux le Vicomte, Maisons-Laffitte, Rueil,
Courances, Chilly, Essones, St Maur, St Mandé, Issy, Meudon,
Chantilly, Verneuil and Liancourt.

He met many of the architects, including probably Mansart
and le Vau, who, as well as working at the Louvre, was building his domed Collège des Quatre Nations (now the Institut de
France) on the Seine's left bank. Above all, he met the great
Bernini, then at the height of his fame, who had been summoned to Paris by Louis XIV to advise on the new Louvre,
and to execute his portrait bust of *Le Roi Soleil*. Wren was
shown Bernini's designs, which "I would have given my Skin
for, but the old reserv'd Italian gave me but a few Minutes
view . . . I had only time to copy it in my fancy and Memory".
But Wren was able to bring back with him many sketches and
engravings—"I shall bring you all France on paper".

There is no documentary evidence that he also studied the
several domed churches then in Paris, but he could not possibly
have missed the dome of the church of the Sorbonne by
Lemercier, the domed church of the Val de Grâce by François
Mansart and Lemercier, and the Italian Guarini's domed
church of Sainte-Anne-la-Royale then nearing completion.
Wren's one and only holiday abroad was indeed an inspiring
working holiday, and from his friend young Edward Browne
we hear that he was hugely impressed by the Seine quays,
which "exceed in all manner of ways the building of the two
greatest pyramids of Egypt"—a tribute which seems too extravagant for Wren himself, and yet he was shortly to be
proposing something similar for London.[14]

In Wren's letter from Paris he refers to the fact that he was preparing "observations on the Present State of Architecture, Arts and Manufacture in France", but it is not known whether he ever completed them. On the other hand, *Parentalia* contains what it calls four "Tracts on Architecture", and also a "Discourse on Architecture" which may have been parts of the preparation for them. None of these essays is complete and they are undated, but they provide valuable evidence of the careful theory upon which Wren's practice was based.

The "Discourse" is very largely an essay on architectural history. He borrows from the Old Testament, Josephus, Pliny and Herodotus in a discussion of Cain's City of Enos, the two columns of the sons of Seth, and Noah's Ark. From Herodotus he describes the Tower of Babel and the Pyramids of Egypt, and discusses the walls of Babylon, the Temple of Solomon, the Pillar of Absalom and the Monument of Porsenna.

In Tract I we have Wren's aesthetic principles clearly stated —architecture not only has a political significance in making "the People love their native country" but it also "aims at Eternity" and is subject to Order rather than to a Fancy which "blinds the Judgment". He echoes Vitruvius' "Strength, Utility and Grace" with his own "Beauty, Firmness and Convenience" as the first principles of sound architecture, and he re-echoes Plato's "the beautiful is that which is pleasing through hearing and sight" by his own "Beauty is a Harmony of Objects begetting Pleasure by the Eye". Wren claimed that there is a "natural beauty" derived from geometry side by side with a "customary beauty" begotten by the use of our senses, and he ranged himself firmly on the side of those who refused to be slavish imitators of the classical past and preferred the freedom of adjusting ancient principles to contemporary needs. Of geometrical figures he prefers the square and the circle, and straight lines are preferable to curves.

In Tract II, Wren discusses the technicalities of the vault and attempts to devise a method for determining the correct abutments to different types. He looks at the various types of vaulting and unhesitatingly decides upon the dome "on pendentives" as the ideal—the method he was finally to use at St Paul's.

In Tract III, the origin of colonnaded streets is considered, and there is much detailed study of such ancient monuments as the Temple of Diana at Ephesus, the Basilica of Constantine and the Temple of Mars Ultor in Rome, and the Mausoleum of Halicarnassus. Apparently, Wren's future practice was based on a more than casual study of the achievements of the past— as always he was a scientist and a theorist before he allowed himself to become a practitioner. It is sad that his work on the Present State of Architecture has not come down to us.[15]

Wren's French visit was fortunately timed—he escaped the worst of the Great Plague of London, described so vividly in the pages of Pepys' diary. On his return to London in the spring of 1666, the plague was on the wane, and Wren found himself immediately concerned in urgent discussions concerning Old Paul's. In 1663 a commission had been constituted to supervise its restoration, and the Surveyor-General, Sir John Denham, supported by John Webb and Edward Marshall the master-mason, had recommended the drastic step of demolishing the remaining steeple and nave, and patching up a smaller compromise from what was left. A shocked commission took further counsel. Roger Pratt reported against demolition, and Wren was then asked for his views. Wren's report—and he had had plenty of time to consider it—was ready in May 1666 soon after his return from France, and the bulk of it is reproduced in Parentalia.[16]

His recommendations were forthright. Let the interior of the nave be re-cased as Inigo Jones had re-cased its exterior, and let it be vaulted with saucer domes, which would be "easy to perform . . . after a good Roman Manner". The remnants of the mediaeval tower should remain for the time being to make easier the eventual construction over the central space of "a spacious Dome or Rotundo, with a Cupola or hemispherical Roof, and upon the Cupola (for the outward Ornament) a Lantern with a Spiring Top should rise proportionately". The old "tower's world of Scaffolding poles" would be invaluable during the course of the new construction, its old masonry would be useful for "filling Stone for the new Work", and Londoners would therefore not be deprived of their usual view of beloved Old Paul's until there was something more impressive to take its place.

Wren followed up his report with his drawings—now at All Souls—for his new St Paul's. They are known as the "pre-Fire" design and are beautifully executed and authentically by his own hand.[17] Their main interest today is in the planning of the dome—an architectural feature which Wren had never seen until his visit to France. The external dome he suggested had affinities with the dome Michelangelo designed for St Peter's at Rome, and the inner dome is close to Lemercier's work at the Sorbonne, while the lofty drum on which the outer dome is placed probably derives from Bramante's contribution to St Peter's. But Wren could never merely borrow and copy—his orthodox wooden lantern was to be surmounted by an open metal-work cone, which may derive from a pine-cone or more probably from the pineapple,[18] which at this period had first arrived from the West Indies and had quickly become the decorative obsession of Restoration builders. Wren's "pre-Fire" design for St Paul's is full of prophetic intelligence, but it is probably as well for his future reputation that his open metal-work cone was never built.

By the time Wren had sent in his report and his drawings, his friend Sheldon had been made Archbishop of Canterbury, and the Dean of St Paul's was William Sancroft, who was also an old friend. In a letter to the Dean, Wren expresses his pleasure in his own proposals—"I shall not repent the great satisfaction and pleasure I have taken in the contrivance which equals that of poetry or compositions in Musick".[19] Happily this somewhat naïve enthusiasm for his own suggestions seems to have been shared by some of the commissioners, and on 27 August 1666, Wren's friend John Evelyn reported that the advocates of "a noble cupola" had "after much contest" at least obtained agreement that "a draught & estimate" should be prepared.[20] It has frequently and mistakenly been maintained that Evelyn reported that the cone design was officially approved.

A week later, the Great Fire of London broke out, and within a fortnight the greater part of the City of London and Old Paul's was in smouldering ruins. It was indeed fortunate for London that at this crisis in her history there was a Savilian professor of astronomy at hand who had already acquired the scholarship, the imagination (and more recently the know-how) to face the consequences of the Great Fire with speed and vision. The stars in their courses had wrought well for the astronomer—he could happily plan a new London, and he could even make a fresh start with designs for a brand new St Paul's.

V

Fire and Phoenix—1666–9

THE GREAT FIRE of London broke out during the night of
Sunday, 2 September 1666, and raged for nearly five days
before it was halted. The resulting ruins, comprising about
seven-eighths of the City including its Guildhall, Exchange,
Customs House, six prisons, 44 livery halls, 87 churches and
Old Paul's cathedral, went on smouldering for weeks. There is a
legend that the fire spread "from Pudding Lane to Pie Corner".
The facts are that it started in Pudding Lane, reached as far
north as the edge of Smithfield and the beginning of Moorfields,
almost as far east as the Tower and as far west as the Temple.
Fortunately, the evidence of two distinguished eye-witnesses
is available—in the diaries of John Evelyn and Samuel
Pepys.[1]

A hot and exceptionally dry summer had left the crowded
inner City of London a more dangerous fire-risk than usual,
and, once the flames took hold, a strong east wind fanned them
to fury, devouring the close-set timber houses and feeding on
the stores of combustible material in the great warehouses.
Evelyn wrote that the catastrophe was "a resemblance of
Sodome", and that "London was, but is no more; the stones
of Paules flew like granados, the lead melting downe the streets
in a streame". He somewhat smugly suggests that the warnings
he had given of the dangers of fire in London in his *Fumifugium*
had indeed been prophetic, and he describes the distress of the
refugees sheltering in temporary tents and shacks beyond the
City's walls. Later, he rode on horseback through the City,
and, forced to dismount at one stage, he tells of how the soles
of his shoes were scorched by the smoking rubbish. At "Old
Paul's" he found "a sad ruine . . . that beautiful Portico (for
structure comparable to any in Europe) now rent in pieces".

The massive blocks of Portland stone in Inigo Jones' Renaissance west front had been "calcined" with the great heat, and the vault of the chancel had crashed down into the crypt-church of St Faith's, where the booksellers and printers of Paternoster Row had taken their stocks of books for safety—they were "burning for a week".[2]

Pepys was both an early observer and a hard-working rescuer. He reported personally to the King, and rightly urged the only method by which the fire could be stopped—by blowing up houses to make gaps over which the flames could not "jump". He was appalled by the havoc, and by the panic of citizens trying to save their goods, and he has a touching thought for the "poor pigeons" which "were loth to leave their houses . . . till they burned their wings and fell down". He, too, refers to the fact that many of the houses "were full of matter for burning", as "pitch and tar . . . and warehouses of oyle and wines and brandy". On 3 September at about four in the morning, Pepys himself could have been seen in his dressing-gown driving his movable goods, his plate, his bags of gold and his papers in a cart to a friend's house at Bethnal Green. His own house—it was in Seething Lane hard by the Tower—was threatened but eventually it just escaped the flames. He was most impressed by the way in which, when the fire finally subsided, most of the citizens coped with their tragedies—"never so great a loss as this was borne so well by citizens in the world", and he quotes with approval the view of a friend that "not one merchant from the 'Change will break upon it".

Perhaps the extent of the devastation can best be gauged by the fact that Pepys reports as late as 17 September that "a sad sight indeed, much fire still in", that his friend Lady Carteret had found "abundance of pieces of burnt papers cast by the wind" as far away as Windsor Forest, and that as late as the following February he carried a drawn sword by his side when he went through the ruins by coach.[3]

On 11 September, less than a week after the fire was under control, Dr Wren presented to Charles II his plan for a new City of London. He was, however, not the only one who imagined that out of the ashes of the fire a new capital might arise, functionally planned and a new wonder of the world. John Evelyn submitted a rival plan two days later, which he

Above : Wadham College, Oxford: Wren's oriel room above the main gateway
Below left : Sundial designed by Wren at All Souls College, Oxford
Below right : Wren's sign language for the deaf and dumb, able to be 'learned in an hour', from *Parentalia*

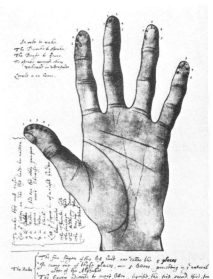

Above: The Sheldonian
Theatre, Oxford, as
originally built

Right: Pembroke
College, Cambridge:
the chapel designed by
Wren 1663–5

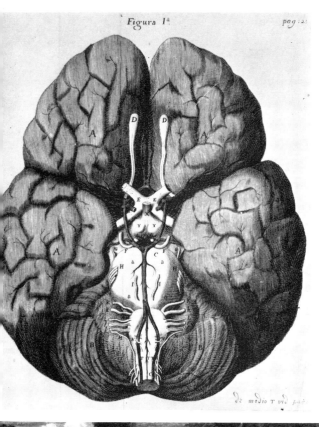

Left: The Brain: Wren's drawing in T. Willis' *Cerebri Anatome . . .*, Geneva 1680

Below: The Custom House, London, designed 1669–74; destroyed by fire 1718

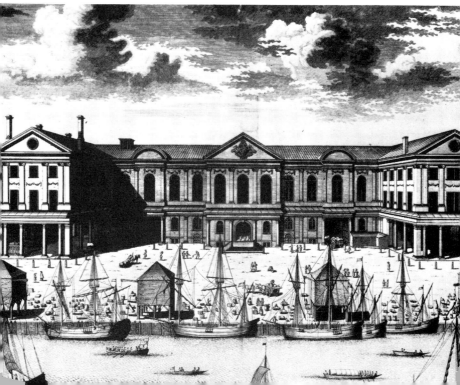

Emmanuel College, Cambridge, 1668–73

Wren's plan for London after the Great Fire of 1666

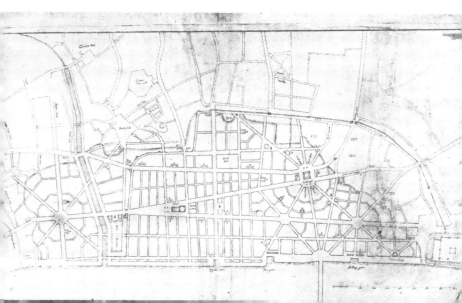

Left: St Mary-le-Bow: Steeple, 1680
Centre: St Magnus the Martyr: Steeple, 1705
Right: St Bride's, Fleet Street: Steeple, 1701–3

St James's,
Piccadilly, 1682–4

St Stephen's,
Walbrook, from
SW Corner,
1672–87

The central space of the Great Model of St Paul's, seen from inside

The Great Model of St Paul's from the NW—Wren's favourite design

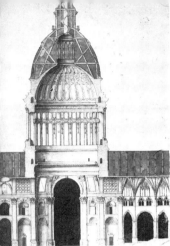

Left: Pre-Fire design for St Paul's, 1666: sectional drawing by Wren

Below: Warrant Design for St Paul's 1675: in section from S, drawn by Wren

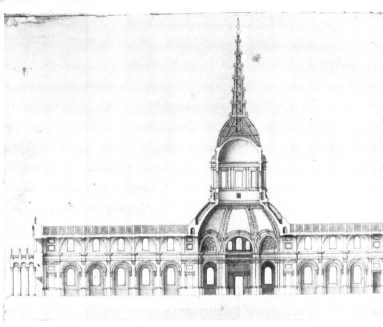

'Penultimate' design for St Paul's, as deduced by Sir John Summerson and drawn by Mrs Leonora Ison

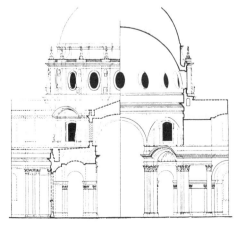

The Crossing at
St Paul's,
looking NW

South Transept of St Paul's, showing Cibber's phoenix in the pediment

Flying Buttresses concealed behind curtain wall at St Paul's, S of choir

Greenwich: Royal Naval College with The Queen's House in the background

Above: Royal Hospital, Chelsea, 1682–91

Right: The Monument, in collaboration with Robert Hooke, 1671–6

Above: A reconstruction engraving of Winchester Palace, 1683–5, from J. Milner's *History of Winchester*, 1798

Left: Tom Tower, Oxford, 1681–2

Fountain Court,
Hampton Court,
from the SE

Hampton Court Palace from the SE, 1689–94

Above: Gateway and Clock Tower of Kensington Palace, 1689–1702

Right: Wren's furniture and carving by Grinling Gibbons in Trinity College Library, Cambridge

Below: Trinity College Library, Cambridge, 1676–84, from Nevile's Court

Above: West Front of St Paul's, showing
Queen Anne Statue

Right: Death Mask, 1723

Portrait by Sir Godfrey Kneller in 1711, when Wren was
nearing eighty

thought captivated the King, the Queen and the Duke of York. A week later, Robert Hooke of Gresham College offered his plan to the City authorities and to the Royal Society, and plans were also submitted to the King by Sir William Petty, Richard Newcourt, and Valentine Knight, of which little is known.[4]

Wren's plan was theoretically attractive. His logical approach made the Exchange and the Cathedral the two major focal piazzas in a rebuilt commercial capital. With the old City gates and London's only bridge determining the approaches, he planned three major arterial roads linking Newgate with the Exchange, the Exchange with St Paul's, and St Paul's with the Tower. The Cathedral ended the vista of the Fleet Street and Ludgate approach—the Ludgate itself was to be replaced by a triumphal arch to Charles II—and the City's churches "with useful Porticos and lofty ornamental Towers and Steeples" were to be re-sited on the main highways. The old Fleet river, which had become a noisome sewer, was to be converted into a clean and navigable canal some 120 feet wide, and, a reflection from his recent Paris visit, there was to be a wide quay along the Thames from the Temple to the Tower. The arterial roads were to be 90 feet wide, the main roads 60 feet wide, and the lesser streets 30 feet wide. And Wren's logic was unsentimental—"all churchyards, gardens, and unnecessary Vacuities, and all Trades that use great Fires, or yield noisome Smells, to be placed out of the Town". His ideal City of London was to be a city, and not a compromise between town and country.[5]

John Evelyn's plan was similar—he may have had previous discussions with Wren on the subject—but it was less inspired. Of the other plans, Valentine Knight's contained the attractive proposal that a navigable canal should run from Billingsgate through Fenchurch Street, Lothbury and Aldersgate to link up finally with a navigable Fleet canal—his touch of Venice-by-the-Thames might have been as attractive as Wren's great piazzas and noble vistas.

Wren's son and grandson began in *Parentalia* the myth that only the selfish obstinacy of the citizens deprived London of a transformation which would have made it one of the most beautifully planned cities in the world, and thoughtless idolators of Wren have since not been slow to perpetuate the myth.

Wren's plan was in tune with many of the contemporary ideas on town planning—he had seen evidence of them in Paris, and especially in the designing by Le Nôtre of the formal gardens at Versailles—but it was not as original as his descendants claimed. An Act of the Commonwealth in 1657 had already decreed that buildings in the City should be of stone or brick, and calls for wider roads and control of smoke and other pollutions had been common ground with all thinking reformers. *Parentalia* alleges that Wren's scheme was accepted by King and Parliament, and only thwarted by the meanness and shortsightedness of the City fathers.[6] The truth is that neither Wren's plan nor any other was officially accepted, and, if Charles II had tried to impose any plan which might have infringed the property rights of the citizens of London, he would more than likely have been sent on his travels again. It must not be forgotten that the fortunes of England at this point in her history were at their lowest ebb.

The Great Plague had carried away 70,000 of London's half-million citizens. It had been followed immediately by the devastations of the Great Fire and then by an exceptionally severe winter. The war with the Dutch had been going badly, and a few months later their guns would be heard at Greenwich, and their ships would break through the boom at Gravesend, burn men-of-war in the Medway and even capture the English flagship. There was no insurance and no compensation for London's refugee citizens—most of them had lived where they worked, and kept their wealth in strong boxes in their homes—and they desperately needed new homes, new offices, new storerooms and a new Exchange with all possible speed. To rebuild in brick and stone, with wider streets and houses designed in terraces without overhanging gables were obvious necessities, but to attempt to dictate a wholesale re-distribution of property was to invite endless controversy and insufferable delay, especially as so much evidence of title had been consumed by the flames. Plans for a revolutionary new pattern of City streets at such a time would be hopelessly unrealistic.

Yet something of good resulted. On 19 September 1666, Charles II proclaimed that the City was to be rebuilt in brick and stone, with wider streets, and six men were named as commissioners for the rebuilding programme.[7] Three were directly appointed by the King—Dr Christopher Wren, Hugh May and Roger Pratt; three were appointed by the City authorities—Robert Hooke, Edward Jerman and Peter Mills. The commissioners were to survey the ruins, and to suggest new legislation for any replanning they recommended. The result was the first Act for Rebuilding the City of London (1667). It gave official approval to the standardization and grading of all new houses in the City—they were to be of brick, of controlled floor-heights and of specified wall-thicknesses. The Fleet ditch was to be converted into a canal and an open Thames-side quay constructed. A tax of one shilling per chaldron (about 30 cwt) on sea-coal was to finance these improvements and to rebuild the City's gaols, but the cost of rebuilding domestic premises was the responsiblity of their owners.

The Act of 1667 superseded the work of the Royal Commission and provided that the City's surveyors should proceed with the rebuilding. For the moment, therefore, Wren was no longer concerned, and planning devolved on Hooke, Jerman and Mills. Unfortunately, Jerman died in 1668. He was succeeded by John Oliver, originally a mason and surveyor and soon to be one of Wren's master-masons and his deputy at St Paul's. Peter Mills was the leading City bricklayer—he had built many houses in the City during the Commonwealth period and also the larger mansion of Thorpe Hall in Huntingdonshire.

Robert Hooke—Wren's life-long friend—was a very formidable character.[8] As an inventor, he made the first spring balance for watches; as a scientist, he introduced freezing point as zero on the thermometer scale, improved the microscope and the telescope, and was the first to describe the cellular structure of plants; as an astronomer, he was the first observer of two stars in Orion's belt; and as a mathematician he could bandy words with Newton and came very close to formulating the laws of gravity. In 1662 he had become the Curator of Experiments to the Royal Society, and he also held the chair of geometry at Gresham College. In his early life he had been apprenticed to the painter Lely, but he had found himself allergic to the odour of paint, and had had to resign. He had a certain gift for architecture based, like Wren's, on his inventive genius, his scientific training and his skill as a draughtsman. He was to be the designer of the new Bethlehem (Bedlam) Hospital, the new Royal College of Physicians, Montague House (where the British Museum now stands) and he was to collaborate with Wren in the designing of the Monument (which he referred to as "the Pillar in Fish Street"). His diary reveals an awkward and rather pathetic genius who suffered from a slight deformity, much ill-health, and a loneliness which his frank liaisons with successive housekeepers did little to ease. From the time he became a City surveyor, he became one of Wren's intimates—sharing his leisure hours, smoking together at the coffee houses, and becoming a friend of the family. *Parentalia* sums him up as Wren's "ingenious and able associate".

And by this time Dr Christopher Wren, though still officially Oxford professor of astronomy, was becoming widely respected as an architect—not least in court circles—and his astonishing appetite for hard, speedy work was beginning to reveal itself. For his friend Dr Bathurst at Trinity College, Oxford, he designed the north wing of the new Garden quadrangle, and it is on this smaller work that we first hear of Thomas Strong the Oxfordshire mason, who, with his brother Edward, was to become one of the master-masons of a new St Paul's.[9] On the other hand, Wren's work at Emmanuel College, Cambridge, was of more consequence, and, although frowned on by architectural purists, it is still a delight to the eye. As was to be his invariable practice, Wren first supplied a model of his design (1667), sent it to the college and only when the model was approved was the work then put in hand. It was for the chapel block of the college—its centre-piece a handsome and imposing composition of large-scale Corinthian half-columns supporting a pediment neatly broken by a square block carrying the college clock with, above it, a pretty domed lantern. The wings are treated more simply, and the whole façade is unified by being carried over an open cloister of classical arcading. It shows the "prentice hand" of the architect of Pembroke and the Sheldonian attempting something more ambitious with great "panache".[10]

The following year (1668) finds Wren doing another Oxford friend a notable favour. Seth Ward, who was his predecessor as Savilian professor, had been appointed Bishop of Salisbury, and he found his great cathedral in sore need of repairs. He asked

Wren to report on the fabric and make recommendations for restorations. The resulting essay in Wren's own handwriting is still to be seen in the library of the cathedral, and it is a very impressive document. He pays generous tribute to the Gothic designers—the proportions of the interior are "decently mixed with large Planes without an Affectation of filling every Corner with Ornaments, which, unless they are admirably good, glut the Eye as much as in Musick too much Division cloyes the Ears". He gave special praise to the windows which let in the maximum light for "nothing could add Beauty to Light". That was a judgement which in later buildings led him to eschew the "dim religious light" of stained glass. But Wren had his criticisms too—chiefly of the engineering, which had not made sufficient allowance for the low and marshy site, and the danger of flooding from the Wiltshire Avon. He made an extremely careful inspection of the magnificent spire, and, although noting with approval the iron bracings within and without, he goes on to a major criticism which he may later have had cause to regret:

> This way of tying Walls together with Iron, instead of making them of that Substance and Form that they shall naturally poise themselves upon Their Butment is against the rules of good Architecture; not only because it is corruptible by Rust, but because it is fallacious . . . for this Reason this Form of Churches has been rejected by modern Architects abroad, who use the better and Roman Art of Architecture.[11]

His recommendations for repairs were prefaced with the typical proviso that he would not "insist upon more expense than necessary", and they were carefully detailed, even giving instructions as to the best way of splicing timber to hold a stretcher and couple walls together. His strengthening of the roof vaulting "by bracing of Iron wrought by Anchor-smiths accustom'd in great Work for Ships—judiciously placed and artfully performed" resulted in a roof which was later declared to be demonstrably stronger than when it was first erected.

Surveys of Salisbury Cathedral in modern times have confirmed that Wren's advice and practice saved a masterpiece, and it is refreshing to find that, where an Evelyn could only rudely refer to the "lame Statues, lace and other Cut-work" of the Gothic, Wren had a proper respect for mediaeval builders, even though he believed them outmoded, and sometimes in error.

Meanwhile, both Archbishop Sheldon and Dean Sancroft had been anxious to retrieve something from the appalling ruins of Old Paul's. They jointly decided to ask Wren to consider whether any general restoration was feasible and specifically whether any part could be adapted for use as a temporary choir until a more complete restoration could be organized.

Once again Wren inspected the ruins, and shortly presented a detailed report and suggestions.[12] He was sceptical of the possibility of a restoration but agreed that there was a possibility of creating a temporary choir out of the old nave. However, the disasters of the naval war against the Dutch postponed immediate action, and it was not until January 1668 that restoration work began. Towards the end of April, Wren, who had gone back to All Souls where he was lecturing on astronomy, received an urgent call for help from Dean Sancroft—"What you whispered in my ear," he wrote, "at your last coming hither is now come to pass. Our work at the west-end of St Paul's is fallen about our ears." He begged Wren to return to London with all speed taking with him "those excellent draughts and designs you formerly favoured us with".[13] Wren readily agreed, and on reaching London he met a Sancroft at last convinced that patching-up Old Paul's would not do, and, refusing a bishopric, the Dean decided to devote himself henceforth to the creation of an entirely new cathedral worthy of London's new glory. And in both Sancroft's and Archbishop Sheldon's mind there was no doubt as to who its architect was to be.

The year 1669 was to be a great year for Dr Christopher Wren. Sir John Denham, the Royal Surveyor, had been ill for many months and was now losing his reason—he died in March. John Webb, who had been Inigo Jones' deputy Surveyor, should have succeeded him—he had in fact been promised the position— and, if Webb was to be ignored, Hugh May was the obvious successor. On 19 March, however, contrary to general expectation, Charles II offered the post of England's chief architect to Wren—and Wren accepted it. Webb, who was approaching 60, was offered the deputy surveyorship in compensation, but in a dignified letter he refused it saying that, although he would have been willing to serve jointly with Wren, he was unwilling to serve under him. He retired, and died three years later. May, whose patron was the powerful Duke of Buckingham, was also disappointed, but not so dignified as Webb. Pepys met him on 21 March in Whitehall and had to listen to a tirade against the Duke's and Charles' ingratitude; May was kept quiet only by an increase of £300 a year in his salary as Comptroller, by various commissions, and later by his extra appointment as Comptroller of the Works at Windsor Castle. Pepys' summing up of the situation was terse but to the point—it was "an ill thing, though Dr Wren is a worthy man."[14]

Christopher Wren in his thirty-seventh year had become Surveyor-General of the Royal Works. If his appointment was unfair to others, it was not a piece of political jobbery and not of his own seeking; and Charles II must be given credit for having preferred promise to performance, and his own shrewdness to protocol. Wren's office was large and his responsibilities great. His salary was a not uncomfortable £26. 8. 4. per month plus expenses (for "riding charges"), and he was provided with a large house as headquarters in Scotland Yard, at that time near Charing Cross. His duties were many and varied—they covered all royal buildings existing or to be planned, and included such minor chores as the designing of State funerals, the preparation of lodgings suitable for a new ambassador and much bureaucratic paper-work. Nevertheless, especially in view of the Great Fire, the surveyorship gave Wren the opportunity of his life, and he seized it avidly.

His first work as Surveyor-General was to give the City a helping hand. The merchants needed a new Customs House as soon as it could possibly be built, and Wren was ready to design it. There are no drawings extant of his plans, but it is recorded that "Mr Wren's Modell" was used, and there is an engraving of 1714 which gives an excellent impression of the resulting building, which was begun in 1669 and finished in five years. The site was a good one—just east of London Bridge on the north bank of the Thames, and it may well be that its Dutch style owed something to the influence of Hugh May. It was a three-sided Renaissance façade enclosing a courtyard facing the river, and plenty of arcaded open-space was provided on the ground floors. Unfortunately, it was burned to the ground five years before Wren's death.[15]

In July of this same year (1669), the new Surveyor-General was invited back to Oxford to witness the grand celebrations at the opening of his Sheldonian Theatre. The ceremonies lasted over two days, and John Evelyn has left a vivid description. Apparently, the Public Orator took the opportunity of making some "malicious & undecent reflections on the Royal Society"—the work of the young *virtuosi* was not welcomed by the older generation of the academic establishment. But Wren himself was duly applauded. He was presented with a gold cup sent by Archbishop Sheldon—the Archbishop himself never saw the theatre he had so munificently given to his old university. A shrewd move of the authorities complimented the architect with the post of perpetual (and honorary) curator of the fabric jointly with the university's Vice-Chancellor.

And it must have been about this time that Wren found time to design a screen for the chapel of St John's College, and also to repair the fan-vaulted roof of the Divinity Schools and to design ingenious hidden extra buttressing for the south side of the Bodleian Library.[16]

Towards the end of the year, Wren, now securely established, sensibly turned his attention to marriage. In the Temple Church, London, he married Faith Coghill, the daughter of Sir Thomas Coghill of Bletchingdon, where Wren had spent so much of his youth with the Holders. Little is known of the first Mrs Wren, but there is one touching memorial of this first marriage—a letter which was written to Faith during their courtship. It has been criticized for its artificiality, but its style is the style of its period, and Wren's whimsical humour smiles through the conventionalities, and his shrewd practicality is well exemplified in its postcript:

Madam, The artificer having never before met with a drowned Watch like an ignorant physician had been so long about the cure that he hath made me very unquiet that your commands should be soe deferred; however, I have sent the watch at last and envie the felicity of it, that it should be so neer your side, and soe often enjoy your eye, and be consulted by you how your Time shall passe while you employ your hand in your excellent workes. But have a care of it, for I put such a spell into it that every Beating of the Ballance will tell you 'tis the pulse of my Heart which labours as much to serve you and more Trewly than the watch; for the watch I believe will sometimes lie, and sometimes be idle and unwilling to goe, having received so much injury by being drenched in that briny bath, that I despair it should ever be a Trew servant to you more. But as for me (unless you drown me too in my teares) you may be confident I shall never cease to be . . . your most affectionate, humble servant, Chr Wren. P.S. I have put the watch in a Box that it might take no harme, and wrapt it about with a little leather, and that it might not jog, I was fain to fill up the corners with either a few shavings or wast paper.[17]

The ill east wind that had fanned the flames of London's Great Fire had guided Wren safely into a position where all his brains and all his strength could now be devoted wholeheartedly to a career which within his own life-time would see, if not his ideal city, at least a better city, and certainly a greater cathedral, rise from the ashes.

City and Cathedral—1670-75

THE SECOND ACT for the Rebuilding of London (1670) trebled the tax on sea coal—1/1½d of the extra 2/- was earmarked for the rebuilding of the destroyed City churches and 4½d was allocated to the reconstruction of St Paul's.[1]

Of the 87 pre-Fire parish churches in London only 52 were to be rebuilt, and various small parishes were amalgamated to this effect. Three commissioners were appointed under the Rebuilding Act—the Archbishop of Canterbury, the Bishop of London and the Lord Mayor of London—but executive authority rested with Wren, who was given the support of three assistant surveyors—his friend Robert Hooke, the mason John Oliver and the surveyor Edward Woodroffe (who had taken the place of the brick-layer Peter Mills who had recently died). There was also the assistance of Wren's very active personal clerk Andrew Phillips.

The procedure for rebuilding gave the initiative to the parochial authorities—they had to obtain a warrant from at least two of the commissioners and then ask Wren for an overall design. The details of the design and the financing of furnishings, altarpieces, fittings, wainscoting, pulpits and fonts could not be a claim on the Rebuilding Funds—the parishes themselves had to meet such expenses. In the surviving parish accounts there are many items which illustrate the normal procedure of the time—they list presents of money, plate or wine to Wren (and sometimes to his lady) and some purposeful hospitality all intended to speed the rebuilding,[2] and in Hooke's diary it is clear that Wren was director and inspirer while his assistants carried out the more humdrum tasks of "viewing" (surveying) and detailed drawing. This combination of centralized overall supervision with parochial freedom in detailing accounts for much of the varied quality in Wren's City churches. In the basic planning, the hand of the master is patently obvious; in the sometimes over-lavish décor there is evidence of a crudity which the master must have deplored. On the other hand, the varied craftsmanship called for in this church designing and furnishing enabled Wren to gather round himself a select group of master craftsmen some of whom were later to be invaluable at St Paul's.

In many ways, Wren's church architecture is more impressive than his work for cathedrals and palaces. He had to devise an entirely new type of church to meet the needs of a Restoration Protestant religion. The only precedents he had were in the work of Inigo Jones in the Chapels Royal and at Covent Garden, and the former were designed for the private use of royal Romanists and the latter was on a special site of little relevance. The only other London church built under the Stuarts was the Laudian Gothic church of St Katherine Cree in Leadenhall Street (1628–31), but Wren was a passionate devotee of the new "Roman" fashion. Where Gothic churches survived, he was quite happy to renovate them in his own version of the Gothic, but, where the Great Fire had gutted them, he seized the opportunity to invent a new kind of church for a new generation of churchgoers. In spite of the license of the Restoration, the Puritan conception of Sunday observance still held. Sunday was a day when attendance at church was obligatory, and both Pepys and Evelyn make it quite clear that the most important furniture of a parish church was not the communion-table but the pulpit. A very secular form of worship called for a new form of ecclesiastical architecture—and Wren supplied it.[3]

It must be remembered that, with very rare exceptions, Wren had to take the sites of the new churches as he found them. In most cases they were hemmed in with tall terraced houses, and distant vistas of their exteriors were rarely possible. It was Wren's typically pragmatic approach which therefore accepted this situation, and concentrated his imagination and inventiveness first on their interiors and later on their steeples.

For sites where there was sufficient space, Wren unhesitatingly adopted the Roman basilican oblong plan with an obtrusive "communion" end, a massive and dominating pulpit, and, where possible, ample side galleries. Where the sites were more awkward, he had the greater fun—let the domes of St Mary Abchurch and St Stephen's Walbrook bear witness to his inspired enjoyment. And, when sufficient funds were ultimately accumulated to cover the cost of steeples, Wren was to create a new London sky-line of infinite variety and soaring beauty which was to entrance Canaletto, and which even the boring bullying tower-blocks in glass and ferro-concrete of twentieth-century London still cannot wholly obliterate.

Architectural critics have indulged their ingenuity and displayed their scholarship in trying to discover the sources of Wren's church designs, and especially in trying to find "originals" for the steeples. We know that Robert Hooke was a great collector of books on architecture, and there was no doubt that Wren read them. We know that Wren himself over his long life amassed an excellent architectural library, and there is a record in the Bodleian Library that in September 1676 his clerk Andrew Phillips was reimbursed for the spending of £3 for a copy of Vitruvius "for the use of the office". It is true that the doorway at the base of the tower of Wren's St Mary-le-Bow bears a strong resemblance to a doorway designed by François Mansart for the Hôtel de Conti in Paris. It is true that the steeple of Wren's St Magnus the Martyr resembles the tower of the Jesuit church at Antwerp, and it may be that the steeple of Wren's St Vedast is reminiscent of Borromini, whom Wren could have studied in his copy of Falda's *Chiese di Roma*. But the mass of Wren's *oeuvre* as a church designer and a steeple-inventor defies denigration by allusion and comparisons. And fortunately there is the evidence of Wren's own memorandum on church building to confirm his theories, and enough surviving Wren churches and steeples to establish his originality.

It should seem vain [he wrote, when further church building was being planned in 1708] to make a Parish church larger than that all who are present can both hear and see. The Romanists, indeed, may build larger Churches, it is enough if they hear the murmur of the Mass and see the Elevation of the Host, but ours are to be fitted for Auditories . . . and all to hear the Service and both to hear distinctly and see the Preacher.

And as for church towers:

> handsome spires, or Lanterns, rising in good Proportion
> above the neighbouring Houses (of which I have given
> several Examples in the City of different Forms) may be
> so sufficient ornament to the Town, without a great expense
> for enriching the outward Walls of the Churches, in which
> Plainness and Duration ought principally, if not wholly, to
> be studied.[4]

Wren's practice often came before his theory—but both
tallied and both were models of invention and common sense.

By the end of 1670, work on thirteen of the new City churches
was well in hand. At St Benet Fink, Threadneedle Street, Wren
devised an original decagon plan, and at this church we first
hear of the famous carver-mason Edward Pierce, who was later
to produce the well-known bust of Wren and contribute brilliantly to St Paul's. And here Wren carried out an early experiment in the designing of a "cupola"—its elliptical dome was
supported by six columns. The church was demolished in 1842
to make way for a new Royal Exchange, but its reredos and
pulpit are preserved in the chapel of Emmanuel School,
Clapham. St Dionis Backchurch, in Fenchurch Street, was a
more traditional design, and since its demolition in 1878 the
quality of its interior can be seen in the fittings that were removed at that time to St Dionis, Fulham. Much of the original
mediaeval fabric of St Christopher-le-Stocks in Threadneedle
Street was restored, but in 1781 it was demolished to make room
for the new Bank of England. At St Dunstan's-in-the-East again
Wren was able to conserve much of the Gothic original, but the
church was destroyed in 1941, and today only its tower remains.
St Edmund, King and Martyr, in Lombard Street, is a very
simple box-like plan with a very elegant and much later octagonal spire. St Mary Aldermanbury was an uncomplicated
Wren design destroyed in 1940, and since exported stone by
stone to the USA. At St Mary-at-Hill the craftsmen of successive
City fathers have been given full rein—it is still one of the City's
most lavish interiors, and there is a shallow dome over the

crossing which was another of Wren's "cupola" experiments. St Mary-le-Bow is justly famed for its steeple, which Wren completed ten years later; but the present interior, grandiose as it is, has little to do with the original Wren designs. St Mary Woolnoth was repaired by Wren, but the whole church was completely re-designed by Nicholas Hawksmoor in 1717. St Michael's, Cornhill, is an original Wren design much altered later by Hawksmoor and Sir Gilbert Scott, so that little of the original remains save a delicate cross-vaulted plaster ceiling. St Mildred's, Poultry, was an undistinguished church demolished in 1872—its simple tower was eighteenth century. Of St Olave's, Old Jewry, only the tower survives—the main fabric was destroyed in 1888. St Vedast, Foster Lane, has a notable Wren steeple, but its interior, apart from some furnishings rescued from other City churches now gone, is modern.

Of the 60 churches in the modern London area for which Wren was the original architect, only 28 remain. Owing to various "developments" during the nineteenth century—for example the building of the new Bank of England, of the Royal Exchange and for the reconstructions connected with the nineteenth-century London Bridge—eighteen original Wren churches were demolished, although some of their internal fittings were redistributed. Of the casualties of the Second World War, eight Wren churches have not been rebuilt although a few of their steeples have been saved, and one ruined church has been sold to and re-erected in the USA. Fortunately, the surviving examples include much of Wren's most impressive work.

But Wren's preoccupation with urgent City business did not prevent his giving attention to the problems of St Paul's. When he had returned from Oxford at Bishop Sancroft's urgent request, he was immediately faced with his life's greatest task. Old Paul's was to be entirely demolished and a new cathedral was to take its place—"a Design handsome and noble and suitable to the Ends of it, and to the Reputation of the City and the Nation", and he was to "take it for granted that Money will be had to accomplish it".[5] Wren's *magnum opus* could begin.

Clearing the site was the first and most prodigious task. The old choir had suffered total collapse, but the massive stump of the great central spire and the Gothic nave, which had been partly "romanized" by Inigo Jones, precariously survived, although Jones' famous western portico had been "calcined" by the flames. It was a very formidable ruin, still dominating the capital, and molten lead cascading from the vaulting had sealed the rubble into solid masses difficult to remove by pick, shovel and wheelbarrow. Wren's ingenuity was equal to the problem. His classical education immediately suggested to him the use of the ancient battering ram. A shaft 40 feet long with a great steel claw at its head was constructed and manhandled by thirty strong labourers.[6] In spite of much incredulity it did excellent service, but the corner bastions of the old tower still refused to yield. Wren resolved on the use of gunpowder, and, with the help of gunnery experts from the Tower, his first attempt at blowing up the ruins was a success. A second attempt had to be left in the care of a subordinate who was less careful, and an exploding stone nearly killed a neighbouring citizen. Wren was therefore compelled to rely only on his battering-ram and traditional methods of demolition.

The chief difficulty remaining was getting rid of the rubbish through the narrow City streets, and finding storage space for stone which could be re-used. But Wren patiently supervised the work from a special office allocated to him in the old Convocation House, and at the same time delegated to Edward Woodroffe and John Oliver the design of a new deanery to house the cathedral authorities. It survives as a modest but very elegant red-brick house to the south of the cathedral with a double gateway (carrying of course pineapple tops) and a high brick wall surrounding a very handsome town mansion. It has never had the esteem it rightly deserves. By the summer of 1670 Wren was ready with a new design for a brand new cathedral.

This second Wren design for St Paul's—the first is the so-called pre-Fire design—is now known as the first model; and it was a strange and almost revolutionary proposal. Instead of the vast Old Paul's, he planned a modest and much smaller structure consisting of a rectangular east end and a domed west end. There still exists at St Paul's a much damaged wooden model of the east end, and one drawing (in private hands) of an elevation, but unfortunately there are no records of what Wren intended for his domed west end. Apparently, the rectangular choir was to be flanked by open external cloisters. For centuries, Londoners had been using the nave of Old Paul's for secular business transactions and public meetings—Wren was providing for this old custom but sensibly excluding it from the inside of the sanctuary. The exterior was to be adorned by Ionic columns for the open arcades and Corinthian columns for the upper storeys. In Wren's 1666 plan for a new City of London after the Great Fire, his St Paul's had shown an outline of just such a new cathedral except that its dome was at the east and not the west end—the reason for the reversal is unknown. In any event, this first model is still a puzzle—it seems unworthy of architect, Church or City, and it may be that it was merely a suggestion for a temporary make-shift until more ample funds permitted a more appropriate scale.[7]

The next stage in the evolution of Wren's St Paul's is even more conjectural, and almost entirely without contemporary documentation. Between October and November 1669 a sum of £50 was paid to William Cleere "for Making the New Model of the Church in Wainscott". In January of the following year, a payment for as much as a hundred guinea pieces was made "to Dr Chr. Wren His Majesty's Surveyor-General and Surveyor also of these Works for his directions and towards drawing and designing a new draught of the whole Church for the Joyners to make a Modell in Wainscott". For this new model William Cleere was paid £200 in April and June 1670.

It has been suggested that the first model was the one which cost £50—it could only have been some six feet long—and that a new and much more elaborate second model (costing £200) was made, based partly on the first model and including its open exterior cloisters, but providing for a choir, a domed central space and nave in the traditional way. This second model needed a posse of porters to carry it from the Convocation House to Charles II at Whitehall, and on 25 November 1672 Hooke records that it received the royal approval, and was duly carried back to St Paul's.

The author of *Parentalia* maintains that his father had now carried out his brief and "contriv'd a Fabrick of moderate Bulk but good Proportion; a convenient Quire with a Vestibule and Porticos and a Dome conspicuous above the Houses, which would have been beautiful and very fit for our Way of Worship, being also a convenient Auditory". On the other hand, Sir Roger Pratt, who saw the second model in July 1673, was forthright in his criticisms—"The two side aisles", he wrote, are "wholly excluded from the Nave of the Church and turned into useless Porticos without, instead of adding a spacious gracefulnesse . . . within", and he was equally scornful of dome, vestibules and elevations. It has been suggested that the second model was intended to be completed in cruciform fashion with the dome at the crossing and a nave extending westwards. It certainly seems inconceivable that Wren could have thought a dome as a vestibule to a choir a worthy and permanent solution for a cathedral to which all Londoners and Englishmen could look forward with hope and pride.[8] And it is even more inconceivable that the humble first model could ever have earned the approval of King Charles II.

But the future of St Paul's was not settled by the royal approval of the second model in 1672. Debate continued, and ecclesiastics and City authorities, while insisting on a cruciform plan, were still not satisfied that Wren had supplied a design for a cathedral church which would be worthy of a great capital city.

> After this [says *Parentalia*] the Surveyor drew several sketches merely for discourse sake, and observing the Generality were for Grandeur, he endeavour'd to gratify the Taste of the Connoisseurs and Cricks with something coloss and beautiful, with a Design antique and well studied conformable to the best Stile of the Greek and Roman Architecture.[9]

The impressive results were, first, what is known as Wren's Greek Cross design of 1672, and, second, his design for the so-called "Great Model" of 1673–4.

The Greek Cross design we know only from its drawings. A dominating central dome is surrounded by an octagon of subordinate spaces, and the outer dome is surmounted by a simple lantern. It was a first revolutionary—too revolutionary—step towards the design of the "Great Model"—which can still be seen at St Paul's.[10]

The Great Model design is substantially the original Greek

Cross design with the additions of an apsed east end and a domed nave carrying a subsidiary lantern. In November 1673, the King appointed a new commission for rebuilding St Paul's in its entirety, and, referring to several designs prepared by his Surveyor-General, he specified "one of which we do more especially approve, and have commanded a Model thereof to be made in so large and exact a manner that it may remain as a perpetual and unchangeable rule and direction for the conduct of the whole Work." The resulting Great Model is a magnificent wooden structure some eighteen feet long and is superbly carried out in great detail with a hatch which enables observers to enter and stand beneath its great dome to obtain a realistic impression of the internal proportions and lighting. Its construction involved twelve joiners, the Serjeant-Painter, many carvers and plasterers all under the supervision of William Cleere the master-joiner—it cost well over £500.

There has been much debate as to whence Wren derived his ideas for this Great Model. The church designs of Leonardo da Vinci; the designs by Bramante and Michelangelo for St Peter's, Rome; the work of Mansart and Bernini for a mausoleum at St Denis; a design for a domed cathedral by either Inigo Jones or his pupil John Webb; the work of Sangallo for the dome of St Peter's—all have been cited as contributing in one way or another to the Great Model for St Paul's. But the model itself exists as Wren's own best advocate. It was certainly original, and definitely something "coloss and beautiful". The great dome—wider than the final structure—was circled by eight saucer domes invisible from outside, a small apse marked the high altar, and at the west end a domed vestibule carried an elegant domed lantern fronted by an impressive portico whose majestic Corinthian columns were to stand 100 feet high. It is a magnificent memorial to Wren's genius.

Robert Hooke records that on 14 November 1673, King Charles conferred the honour of knighthood on his Surveyor-General.[11] It must have been some slight compensation to Wren for the early death of his first son Gilbert in March of this same year, and it is probable that the bust of Wren, now in the Ashmolean museum at Oxford, carved by his mason Edward Pierce, was commissioned at this time. It is a brilliant example of realistic sculpture—thanks to it we know very exactly what

Wren was like in his prime, with his wide-awake eyes set in an
ascetic face, with a faint smile playing round the lips and a
profusion of curly hair—all expressive of the energy and fire
which must have been in the man now happy at last to resign
his Savilian professorship of astronomy and to devote the whole
of his future energies to his new career as royal architect.

Unfortunately, even the royal approval and Wren's own
preference could still not prevail against the conservatism of the
cathedral authorities. As *Parentalia* puts it, the Great Model
pleased "Persons of Distinction, skill'd in Antiquity and Architecture", but the Cathedral Chapter thought it "not enough of
a cathedral fashion", and complained that it could not be built
by stages in usable parts.[12] There is no doubt that in the Great
Model we still have Wren's favourite design, and there is an
apocryphal story that, when it was ultimately rejected, he wept:
it has certainly remained the favourite design of most architectural critics ever since. Wren was compelled once again to go
back to his drawing-board.

It is a sad story with a puzzling sequel. Wren turned to his
several previous drawings for traditional cruciform and basilican designs, and finally produced the design now known as the
"Warrant Design" because it was stitched to the definitive royal
warrant dated 14 March 1675. The warrant ordered an
immediate start to building in accordance with its affixed
design.

Wren was both exasperated and bitterly disappointed by the
final rejection of his Great Model. His son maintained that
"the Surveyor resolved to make no more models, or publickly
to expose his Drawings", and "he turned his thoughts to a cathedral form (as they called it) but so rectified as to reconcile as
near as possible the Gothick to a better manner of architecture,
with a cupola and above that, instead of a lantern, a lofty spire
and large porticoes".[13] This was the Warrant Design of 1675—
an almost ludicrous caricature forced on the architect by con-
flicting pressures. A cruciform Gothic cathedral is disguised in
"Roman" trimmings, and its centre-piece is a double shallow
dome surmounted by a lofty Renaissance spire, very much as
though St Bride's "wedding-cake" steeple were perched high
above a dome of more normal proportions. It is possible that
this was a deliberate *reductio ad absurdum* of what the clergy

demanded, and Wren had the wisdom to obtain from Charles II himself "the liberty in the prosecution of his work to make variations, rather ornamental than essential, as from time to time he should see proper".[14] It was a liberty which Wren was to stretch to the full—the Warrant Design was never executed, and was possibly never intended to be executed.

On 18 June 1675, the first contracts for a new St Paul's were at last signed. Joshua Marshall, master-mason to the crown, and Thomas Strong, mason and Oxfordshire quarry-owner, had already been working for the Surveyor-General on some of his new City churches—they were now enlisted to begin a greater work. And it was while they were all "setting-out" the site for the new choir that Wren called to a labourer to bring him a piece of stone to use as a marker—it was a fragment from a wrecked tomb, and on it Wren saw but one word—*Resurgam* (I shall rise again).[15] It was a happy omen after months of frustration, and on 21 June of this same year, nine years after the Great Fire, the foundation stone of the new St Paul's was laid, without ceremony but in the presence of the master-masons, at its south-eastern corner.

And while St Paul's had been the Surveyor's major pre-occupation he had not neglected his duty to the City churches. At St Stephen's, Walbrook, begun in 1672, he had designed his most exciting church interior—the crowded site made a lavish exterior pointless. The interior was a magical surprise—a semi-circular dome richly coffered was balanced on eight arches carried on as many slender Corinthian columns, and eight more supported the side-vaulting. Wren designed it for box-pews to the height of the bases of the columns. The reredos, organ case and pulpit were all of excellent quality thanks to the patronage of the wealthy Grocers' Company. It is not surprising that the masons were Edward Strong and Christopher Kempster, that the carpenter was John Langland and the wood-carver Jonathan Maine, all of them were to find even greater scope for their great talents in the new cathedral. The church-wardens voted "twenty Guineas in a silk purse" to Wren "or his Lady" for his great care "and extraordinary pains in contriving the design and assisting in the rebuilding". Wren was not overpaid —St Stephen's, Walbrook is a minor masterpiece, and solving the problems of its dome must have been of great help to Wren when he approached the greater problems of the "cupola" for his cathedral.

In 1674, the restoration of two more City churches had been begun. At St Bartholomew Exchange was a modest church of no great interest save for an excellent reredos. In 1840 the church had to make way for the new Royal Exchange, but the reredos was moved to St Giles Cripplegate where it did not survive the bombing of 1940. At St Stephen's, Coleman Street, Wren planned a simple hexagonal interior superimposed by a pleasant lantern steeple, but after many alterations and unkind restorations it was finally destroyed by German bombs and not restored.

It was also in 1674 that Wren was concerned with three other minor architectural projects. In 1674 he constructed a new Drury Lane theatre for Thomas Killigrew the dramatist and Master of the Revels to Charles II, of which little is known, and which was later unrecognizably altered by Robert Adam.[16] In 1674–5, Wren and Hooke were jointly concerned in building a new Navy Office in Seething Lane.[17] And in 1674 Wren contributed to the Honeywood library at Lincoln Cathedral—a very simple building carried on a light arcading of Tuscan columns. It is possible that Wren's function was mainly advisory —the contract for the building speaks of Wren's "directions" but of a "Mr Thompson's model".[18]

It was at this time, too, that Wren first attempted to enter politics—rather half-heartedly it seems. He offered himself as a candidate for his old university and had the support of the King, but he does not seem to have been too distressed when he was defeated by a candidate more convivial in his electioneering tactics.

On the threshold of his middle age, Sir Christopher Wren could feel that he had finally chosen wisely in preferring architecture to astronomy. True, his favourite design for St Paul's had been turned down, but he had been given a free hand with the selected design, his work for the City churches was progressing excellently, and interesting external commissions were on the horizon.

Frustrations and Achievements—1675–85

IN FEBRUARY of 1675 a second son was born to the Wrens and christened Christopher—he survived and lived to the age of 72. Unfortunately, in the following September Lady Wren contracted the then very prevalent disease of smallpox and did not recover. It was perhaps fortunate that Wren himself at this time was very fully occupied with his new career.

As the City slowly revived, a new landmark appeared above the new house-tops. By the instructions of the first London Rebuilding Act of 1667, the Surveyor-General had had to produce a suitable monument to commemorate the Great Fire. Of the drawings for this memorial which still remain none is from Wren's own hand, and it seems that Robert Hooke was largely responsible for them. Designing had begun in 1671, and in Hooke's diary for 19 October 1673, he records that he had "perfected module of Piller" and one of his drawings carries Wren's official counter-signature of approval.

The "Monument", as it has been known ever since, was undoubtedly a work of collaboration between the two friends.

In style, it was an exercise in classical archaeology resulting, after some debate, in a fluted Roman Doric pillar surmounted by a flaming gilded urn, and an exterior viewing-balcony reached by an internal staircase. To the suggestion that a large phoenix should surmount the pillar, Wren objected, with typical common sense, that it would be "costly, not easily understood at that highth, and worse understood at a distance, and lastly dangerous by reason of the sayle the spread wings will carry in the winde". Apparently Wren was also unhappy with the final choice—it was the King's—of an urn; Wren had a hankering either for a statue of the King, or for brass symbolic flames bursting from the sides of the pillar surmounted by a *small* phoenix. On its massive square base, Caius Gabriel Cibber, the Danish sculptor who was also to work for Wren at St Paul's and Hampton Court, carved a rather forced allegory in stone haut-relief depicting Charles II in Roman armour directing the succour of a distressed Lady London. The sensible original inscription stated that the Monument had been built "the better to preserve the memory of this direful visitation", but later, as a consequence of the Popish Plot of 1678, the origin of the Great Fire was attributed to the Papists and a revised inscription maintained that the Fire was "begun and carried on by the treachery and malice of the Popish faction". Naturally, under the Romanist James II this was obliterated, but under Protestant William and Mary it was re-engraved and not finally removed until 1830. It constrained Pope to write the satirical lines:

> Where London's column pointing to the skies
> Like a tall bully, lifts the head, and lies.

And there was a second lie. "In three short years" ran the Monument's inscription in reference to the rebuilding of the City, "the World saw that finished which was supposed to be the work of an age". In fact, the City of London was dotted with ruins for another twenty years.[1]

The Monument is scarcely an artistic masterpiece, and its balcony has not been improved by its modern anti-suicide cageing, but it has continued down the years to give successive generations of Londoners and London's visitors an impressive panorama of the capital. Its mason was the Joshua Marshall who was to work for Wren at St Paul's, and who was also responsible for some of Wren's City churches. It still provides the best view, in spite of latter-day tower-block developments, of St Paul's and of Wren's surviving City churches.

A minor contribution to the London scene was made in 1675, when it was decided to erect at Charing Cross an equestrian statue of Charles I which had been cast by the Huguenot sculptor Hubert le Sueur as far back as 1633. The statue was originally commissioned by Lord Treasurer Weston for his garden, but on the outbreak of the civil war it had not been delivered and had remained in the sculptor's foundry. After the King's execution, the parliamentarians sold the statue for melting down, but its royalist buyer buried it instead, and at the Restoration revealed his loyalty. Wren made several drawings for its pedestal, and it seems likely that one of them was carved by Joshua Marshall according to a contract dated 2 July 1675. Although its stone has weathered badly, it is still a decorative base well worthy of one of the very few good public statues in London.[2]

In the same year, Wren was closely concerned with a building at Greenwich now known as Flamsteed House.[3] It was the first royal observatory to be built in England, and it was designed by Wren for Charles II, who wished to install there John Flamsteed as his first Astronomer-Royal. As an astronomer himself, Wren must have relished this commission. He seems to have revelled in a composition of small domes and turrets resulting in a romantic brick house with a great octagonal observation room on its first floor and a décor more Jacobean than Roman. When Wren, some six years later, was building Tom Tower at Oxford for Dean Fell, who was wanting to incorporate a telescope, Wren wrote to him and observed "wee built indeed an Observatory at Greenwich not unlike what your Tower will prove: it was for the Observator's habitation, and a little for Pompe".[4] It was a good description for his Royal Observatory, Flamsteed House.

In the following year (1676), Wren was able to be of service to his old friend and Gresham colleague, the geometrician Dr Isaac Barrow, who was now the Master of Trinity College, Cambridge. Barrow had become involved in an academic controversy in which he had advocated the building of a Senate House on the lines of and for the same purposes as Oxford's Sheldonian Theatre. Barrow turned to Wren for help, and the Surveyor promptly produced a design for a large arcaded hall and a large library for the university—it would have been rather a dull undistinguished pile to judge from the drawings. But, in the event, this scheme was turned down, and in some dudgeon Barrow decided to confine his building ambitions to his own college. He asked Wren to design for him a new college library, and Wren accepted with enthusiasm.

His first design for Trinity's library showed a square exterior surmounted by an impressive dome, fronted by a portico of Roman Ionic columns and a pediment. It has been suggested, with more than usual likelihood, that in general this was derived from Palladio's original design for his famous Villa Capra at Vicenza. For some unknown reason, this attractive if borrowed plan was abandoned, and, in February 1676, Wren's second design began to take shape. Wren sent his drawings to Dr Barrow together with a long explanatory letter which still exists.

The library block was to complete Nevile's Court, which already had side-blocks with arcaded first storeys open to the courtyard. Wren explained that in continuing a similar arrangement for his library block it would be "according to the manner of the ancients who made double walks . . . about the forum". His new library block was to have "open walks" but on a grander scale, and the resulting courtyard façade illustrated Wren's unorthodox ingenuity to perfection. He wanted an interior which would provide the maximum shelf-room for books and ample window lighting for the readers, and at the same time he wanted an open loggia to link the new block with the existing arcades of the other sides of the courtyard. His solution was to design a first storey of Doric pillars supporting a bold architrave with semi-circular arches, but the arches were filled in with carved lunettes so that the openings were the same height as those of the existing sides. The floor of the library was not at the level of the architrave (where it appeared to be from the outside) but at the level of the springing of the arches. It was an illusionist device which gave him very large glazed semi-circular windows, extra space for shelving and furniture, and, outside, a second storey of Ionic columns to support a bold roof balustrade embellished only with four statues in the centre and shallow domed pavilions at each end. Dr Barrow was apparently slightly shocked by the architect's daring, but Wren reassured him—he had seen "the effect abroad in good buildings"—probably a reference to le Vau's Collège de France which he had seen on his visit to Paris.

Wren took elaborate pains with the interior—the bookcases were arranged longitudinally and also at right angles to the walls in order to create bays for quiet study, and he even designed the stools and book rests. In order to provide for the great weight of the loaded bookshelves, he used an ingenious beam-system which he had also used for strengthening Duke Humphrey's Library at the Bodleian at Oxford. And at last he was able to redeem a promise he had made to John Evelyn some five years before.

Evelyn had invited Wren to dine at his house in Deptford, and after dinner he had taken Wren to meet a young wood-carver named Grinling Gibbons who was working in a small thatched cottage not far away. When Evelyn and Wren arrived, Gibbons was busy on an intricate representation in wood of Tintoretto's "Crucifixion". Wren was duly impressed and pro-mised to use the young Gibbons as soon as an opportunity occurred—and Evelyn records that Gibbons still spoke in the Dutch accent he had picked up while training as a wood-carver in Holland. Now the opportunity had come. Wren com-missioned Gibbons to carve all the decorative panelling, and the busts on the bookcases for Trinity College Library—they are masterpieces.

The exterior of the library facing the river is a much plainer affair. It is a somewhat grim though dignified closed wall—it shuts the college in; and, no doubt, if Wren could have foreseen the modern creation of "The Backs", he might have devised a walling a little less dour and forbidding. Yet externally and internally Trinity College library illustrates Wren at his best and most typical—never hidebound to orthodoxy, ever prac-tical in solving a practical problem, and yet achieving pro-portion, dignity and style.[5] And it is interesting that Wren seems to have built his library very much by correspondence—either with Barrow or with Robert Grumbold the master-mason. There is no record of Wren visiting Cambridge.

And while busy on Trinity library, Wren still found time to begin work on three more City churches. At St James, Garlick Hill in Upper Thames Street, the great Oxfordshire mason Christopher Kempster carried out a sober but impressive basilican plan with a fine vaulted ceiling lit by an upper range of plain windows, graceful Ionic fluted pillars and much excel-lent craftsmanship in wood and iron. At St Michael's Bassi-shaw, again a simple basilican plan was adhered to and the exterior had Dutch affinities. The whole church was demolished in 1888. St Michael's, Queenhythe, was another unpretentious church, but it contained some of the early work of the great woodcarver Jonathan Maine. The church was demolished in 1876 but some of the fittings including Maine's pulpit, were removed to St James, Garlick Hill.

In February of the following year, Wren remarried. The new Lady Wren was Jane, daughter of William, Lord Fitzwilliam of Lifford; and it was perhaps a sign of Wren's growing importance that the wedding was solemnized in the Chapel Royal of St James's Palace. In November, Lady Wren presented the Surveyor with a daughter, Jane, of whom he was to become passionately fond.

1677 saw nine more City churches on the way to complete renovation. All Hallows, Watling Street, because of its site, was a simple if irregular oblong with no great pretentions but with some excellent examples of the great work of John Langland, master-carpenter, and William Cleere, master-joiner. It was demolished in 1876–7. All Hallows-the-Great, Upper Thames Street, was another oddly-shaped rectangular church handicapped by its site. It was demolished in 1893–4 but its screen, sounding board, communion table and pulpit were distributed to other London churches. St Anne and St Agnes in Gresham Street is a homely red-brick design with a surprising interior— a shallow central dome is supported on four Corinthian columns. It has some excellent woodwork. St Benet, Paul's Wharf, betrays Dutch influences, and its interior is less disturbed than most of Wren's City churches. Its galleries remain, its columns spring from gallery level, and the pulpit, fittings and furnishings are all typical examples of elaborate if rough seventeenth-century craftsmanship. The church is now the church of the Welsh-speaking members of the Church of Wales. The interior of Christ Church, Newgate Street, was gutted in 1940, and it was a sad loss. It was a galleried basilican design with a fine coved roof supported on Corinthian pillars springing from bases to gallery level. Fortunately, the steeple remains. At St Martin's, Ludgate, just below the new cathedral, Wren devised a tiny church with a surprisingly splendid interior of impressive Corinthian columns supporting a fine barrel-vaulted roof from whose centre is suspended a superb and elaborate chandelier. At St Mildred's, Bread Street, Wren again experimented with a shallow dome. Unfortunately, the church was totally destroyed in 1941. There is at St Peter's, Cornhill, a rare example of a Wren chancel screen, and its eastern wall also gave him the chance to produce one of his most interesting exteriors. At St Swithin's, Cannon Street, a Wren masterpiece was destroyed in 1941. Its exterior showed Italianate motifs, and its interior a dome over an octagon which was yet another experiment in designing "cupolas".

1677 also saw a start to the building of Abingdon Town Hall. It is a very distinguished achievement, and, although there is no documentary proof, it has frequently and understandably been attributed to Wren. It was certainly built by one of his masons, Christopher Kempster, and, in recommending him as one whom he had "used in good workes" Wren mentions that he "wrought the Town house at Abbington".[6]

In January 1678 Parliament voted £70,000 for a solemn second funeral for the martyr-king Charles I, and for a monument "for the said Prince of glorious memory". The Surveyor-General therefore designed a cylindrical mausoleum which was to be erected at Windsor, and its resemblance to Bramante's famous Tempietto at S. Pietro in Montorio at Rome is too close for it to be doubted that here for once he unashamedly borrowed from an Italian master. Inside, he planned a sculptured group, and twenty statues were to circle the lower cylinder. The upper cylinder was to be capped by a miniature reproduction of Michelangelo's design for a dome for St Peter's. Unfortunately, nothing more was heard of the project—presumably because the actual cash was never forthcoming—and all that remains are Wren's superb drawings.[7]

Only one City church was begun in this year—the very interesting St Antholin's, Watling Street. Its interior was an ingenious design for so awkward a site—a shallow dome was supported on an octagon of Corinthian pillars on high plinths. It was a scandal that so noble an interior was demolished in 1874.

Meanwhile, progress at St Paul's was steady if not spectacular. On Wren's recommendation, masonry contracts were shared between two master-masons—Joshua Marshall, master-mason to the crown and the son of a mason-sculptor who had worked for Inigo Jones, and Thomas Strong, whose family owned stone quarries at Taynton in Oxfordshire, and who, thanks to relaxed regulations since the Great Fire, had built up a thriving business in stone at a site close to Paul's Wharf. There were some sixty journeymen working for the two master-masons, and over 100 labourers levelling, mortar-mixing, and fetching and carrying for their masters. At the north-eastern corner of the site it was found necessary to dig down twenty feet or more to the London clay to be sure of firm foundations, but, in spite of such temporary setbacks, the walls and piers of the crypt were finished and the shape of things to come made clearer.

Wren's position at the centre of all this activity called for organizational powers of the highest order—stores, payments, contracts, discipline, designs and *esprit de corps* were all included in his direct responsibility, and he was even personally concerned in coping with the constant pilfering which went on. He built a spiked rubble wall round the entire site, and engaged two watchmen assisted by watchdogs to patrol the area at night —we still have signed accounts for the dogs' meat, and at one period for veterinary treatment for the largest dog.[8] Overall control was combined with scrupulous attention to detail. And the magnitude of Wren's task must have worried the commissioners. Wren's initial fee was a very modest £100 per annum —they raised it to £200; and would have gone higher if Wren had so wished.

A few months after the laying of the St Paul's foundation stone, Wren had suffered the great loss of one of his assistant-surveyors—Edward Woodroffe. Fortunately, he was able to persuade the very efficient but elderly John Oliver—he was 60 —to take his place, and it turned out to be a wise and successful appointment. At Child's coffee house hard by the cathedral site Oliver, Hooke and Wren found a congenial and quiet refuge from the noise and tumult of the building site.

In October 1675, Wren had been fortunate in that an old friend became Bishop of London. He was Henry Compton, who had accompanied him on some of his explorations round Paris, ten years before, and who, after serving in the Guards, had taken holy orders, and, thanks to the influence of his brother the Earl of Northampton and his patron Lord Derby, had become Bishop of Oxford. According to John Evelyn, he was not much of a preacher, but "a most sober, grave and excellent prelate", and he soon proved himself a very good friend to Wren and to St Paul's.[9]

The finances of the new cathedral were in a precarious state. The coal dues at the $4\frac{1}{2}$d rate authorized by the Act of 1670 were only bringing in some £4,000 to £5,000 a year, and private benefactions were scarce.[10] On 5 July 1677, the commissioners called a general meeting to discuss the financial crisis, and Bishop Compton was of course present. The balance sheets proved that in seventeen years the coal dues had produced £24,500, the sale of old materials a mere £836, and private gifts and legacies a total of £16,000. It was clear that a national appeal for funds was urgently required. The King sent letters to all cities, towns and parishes, and Bishop Compton produced an eloquent pamphlet which justified London in asking for national help. The results were rewarding. Cities, universities, churches and other cathedral chapters responded generously, and smaller donations flooded in from every rank of society. Even the building officials at St Paul's contributed—Wren himself contributed £60 and Oliver £50, and a new custom was established whereby for certain church appointments the new holder had to make an obligatory contribution of £10 to the St Paul's funds.

In November 1677 Archbishop Sheldon died—but his successor, to everyone's surprise, was Sancroft, Dean of St Paul's, and Wren was delighted. One of the new Archbishop's first acts was to obtain an Order-in-Council which ensured that, instead of giving gloves to guests at consecration dinners, all bishops in future were to contribute £50 to the St Paul's building fund.[11] Sancroft's successor as Dean of St Paul's was also an old friend of Wren's—Dr John Tillotson, who had been Dean of Canterbury and who was also a Fellow of the Royal Society. And, to complete a rosier future for the Surveyor, his own brother-in-law, Dr William Holder, was at this time appointed to a vacant St Paul's canonry. Holder's wife, Susan, was, as we have noted, Wren's favourite sister, and Wren became a frequent visitor at the Holders' new house in Amen Corner.

Meanwhile, the success of Bishop Compton's national appeal made possible an annual expenditure of between £10,000 and £14,000 a year for a further six years, and, on the strength of this security, Wren, in 1679, ordered work to begin on the foundations of St Paul's nave. Yet to the ordinary Londoner work at St Paul's seemed inordinately slow—even the choir walls were not yet as high as the roof of the neighbouring houses. And to add to the Surveyor's worries there was trouble at the royal quarries on the Isle of Portland whence came the pearly white limestone which Wren demanded for his cathedral's exterior.

The so-called Isle of Portland on the Dorset coast was Crown property, and its quarrying industry was regulated by a code peculiar to itself. There were approximately 700 "islanders" who had the right to quarry, but, if they wished to send quarried stone away, permission had to be obtained from the Surveyor-General, and Wren on his appointment had very wisely had this regulation confirmed. In Inigo Jones' day, a new pier had been built and new roads, tracks and cranes had been kept in good order, but during the civil war period the island's industrial amenities had been neglected and misused, and Wren was faced with a dissatisfied labour force and the need for considerable repairs to installations. He had reported to the King in December 1675, and in the following February his proposals had received royal approval. The commissioners appointed a well-known City stone merchant, Thomas Knight, as their agent on the island, and all seemed well. The quarried stones were horse-driven to the piers, and soon there were six ships regularly plying between London and the island carrying loads of over 150 tons. Below London Bridge the stones were transferred to lighters and barges and duly delivered at Paul's Wharf. From the wharf to the actual cathedral site was a steep short journey made more difficult by the narrow streets and busy traffic.[12] For the interior of his cathedral Wren did not need the hard and expensive Portland stone—he used the famous Caen stone, Beer stone from Devonshire, limestone from the Strong quarries near Burford and at Taynton; and frequently Headington stone from Oxford, Kentish ragstone from Maidstone, ashlar from Reigate and Guildford were also called in aid.

With raw materials assured, and with the site cleared, the

basic outlines of a new cathedral could be dimly seen through the forest of scaffolding. But these outlines were not the outlines of the Warrant Design—Wren had lost no time in taking full advantage of the King's special licence. From the moment the foundation stone was in place, it must have been clear at least to the master-masons that radical changes were on the way. And the processes by which the absurdities of the Warrant Design of May 1675 were eliminated, and by which Wren, some 36 years later, saw his *chef d'oeuvre* completed are as fascinating as they are sometimes obscure.[13] Surviving drawings are plentiful, but their datings, and sometimes even their precise authorship, are indecisive. Throughout, Wren was keeping his own counsel, taking the fullest advantage of his royal licence to make alterations, and deciding for himself whether his amendments were either "ornamental" or "essential", or both.

First, the "warranted" ground-plan was altered. Its traditional cruciform shape had provided, as was customary in a Gothic cathedral, for a choir shorter than the nave and transepts of lesser, but of course of equal length. Wren, keeping closely but not precisely to the same basic area, now decided to add greater emphasis to the central space at the "crossing". He therefore planned a nave of exactly the same length as the choir, but with its west end increased by an extra bay of greater proportions having on either side a chapel, and so giving added importance to the entrance portico and its twin towers. At the same time he reduced each transept by a bay and compensated for this by providing elegant elliptical pillared entrances to each of them. The story that it was the Catholic James, Duke of York, who insisted upon the two side chapels, with a view to a return to Romanist forms of worship, cannot be substantiated—it is much more likely that they were an expression of Wren's consistent policy of reversing the traditional emphases of the Gothic. He was not so much interested in the priestly rituals of choir and high altar, but he was concerned with great State occasions and great popular assemblies. It was for these that he was planning his great "cupola" and his majestic entrance hall.

The second change was more radical. The Warrant Design's wedding-cake steeple was promptly abandoned, and no-one either then or since has regretted it. It was replaced by a simple dome resting on a drum pierced by sixteen oval windows. For reasons which seem obscure, it was at this stage that Wren now decided to increase the width of the outer walling by reducing the width of the aisles in the Warrant Design, thus creating for himself a difficult future problem in covering the central space.[14] The Warrant Design at least had the merit that it provided a central space which could be supported on an octagon with arches of equal calibre. Wren was now committed to a future design in which the four diagonal arches over the sides of his octagonal central space would be shorter than the four main arches over choir, transepts and nave.

In a design which has come to be known as the Penultimate Design—thanks to a brilliant exercise in reconstruction by Sir John Summerson made from various drawings which have recently come to light[15]—Wren first solved his "crossing" problem by inserting a large window in each of the shorter diagonal bays so as to achieve a dramatic oblique lighting for the central space. But there were further difficulties. This Penultimate Design had the serious drawback that its central dome would have been little more than 200 feet high, whereas clergy, City, court and citizens were expecting to see something far more impressive dominating the new City skyline. The spire of Old Paul's had once been 500 feet high; Wren's own Great Model had promised a dome of some 300 feet; the new St Paul's must at least be no less. Even while his masons were already at work on foundations, crypt and ground courses, Wren had once again to rethink his ideas for the final superstructure, and at the same time ensure that the preliminary building could provide for it. His solution was both original and fundamental, and no-one knows exactly when he arrived at it—it has aroused controversy ever since.

The external walls of both the Warrant and the Penultimate Designs reached in the usual Gothic manner no higher than the height of the aisles—much lower than the height of the main vaulting. Wren, without in any way affecting the new basic plan, now determined to add screen walls standing on top of the strengthened exterior aisle walls round the whole building, and reaching to the maximum height of the future main saucer-domed roofing. With one brilliant, if unorthodox, amendment, he obtained at least three overwhelming benefits.

His prime objective was—it always had been—a central dome of truly colossal proportions. Now he could replan his "cupola" to an impressive height, and take care of the resulting extra pressures by the extra weight and stabilizing effects of the heightened walling. Now, his enforced Gothic plan could ultimately carry a Roman dome riding securely at the centre of what would appear from the outside to be a proportionately massive Roman basilica the full height of its vaulting. Now, behind the heavy screen walls he could construct and conceal those flying-buttresses for the better support of domes and roofing which were a part of the Gothic tradition he respected but which, if they were to be visible, would scarcely be in keeping with the Roman décor on which he was determined.[16]

There is an authenticated Wren drawing, almost certainly of 1675 or early 1676, which shows these heightened screen walls with their lavish carvings and illusionist blank windows (or "tabernacles"), at each transept a graceful elliptical porch, and soaring above it all a dome of truly impressive proportions not unlike Michelangelo's design for St Peter's in Rome. Wren was still not clear in his own mind as to the detailing of the central dome, nor indeed had he finally decided on the shape of the twin western towers—at this early stage they were almost replicas of Bramante's tempietto at S. Pietro in Montorio at Rome. But in the meantime his masons could continue completing the main walls and columns secure in the knowledge that a great dome and western towers—whatever their final detailing—could be safely accommodated. Critics have not been slow to condemn Wren's unorthodox illusionism as an unworthy sham—most observers nowadays are happy to admire it as the brilliant contrivance of genius.

There were further alterations to the Warrant Design, and there were new problems connected with the central space still to be solved, but St Paul's was now growing slowly and steadily under Wren's guiding hand and the many thousands of visitors who inspected his Great Model, which was on show in the Convocation House, must still have been under the impression that the model was an accurate representation of their future cathedral. It was another twenty years before even Wren himself was quite sure of the final picture.

Meanwhile, in spite of his major responsibility for St Paul's and his obligation to the City authorities, Wren still found time for other projects as well as for the routine chores of his royal office.

In 1679, he became a member of the council of the Hudson's Bay Company, and for five years he was one of its active directors, and of course, a shareholder. He was a regular attendant at company and committee meetings (he received 6/8d for each attendance providing he was prompt in arriving). Until his death in 1682, Prince Rupert was the Governor, and he was succeeded by the Duke of York—afterwards James II—and Wren was frequently called upon to act as deputy Governor. Wren was naturally consulted when the company was renting or buying property, but he was equally involved in matters of less moment—it is recorded that the bolts and locks at the company's warehouses should be affixed "as Sir Chr. Wren shall judge fitt to be done".[17]

But 1679 brought Wren private sorrow—his third son William was born mentally retarded and for the greater part of his life—he lived to almost 60—he was in the care of his elder brother Christopher.

In the following year, the Benchers of the Middle Temple commissioned Wren to design a cloistered set of buildings for Pump Court. Wren's original design provided for a cloister of seven arches but in fact the finished building had eight. Unfortunately, it was another Second World War casualty, and only photographs remain.[18]

And Wren was not neglecting his churches. There is evidence that he was concerned with the church of St Anne's in Soho, but the fabric did not survive the bombing of 1941, and its steeple (which remains) was designed by William Talman in 1714 and rebuilt by S. P. Cockerell in 1802. At St Augustine's, Watling Street, Edward Strong was the mason, and Jonathan Maine the carver of a very simple rectangular design—it also was destroyed in 1941. At St Clement Danes, Strand, Wren's original work was another wartime casualty, but its well-known steeple (which survives) was the work of James Gibbs. And the steeple of St Mary-le-Bow in Cheapside was also completed in this year—it displayed Wren at his superlative best. Its design is one of his most complicated exercises, and the fact that it survived the bombing of the rest of the fabric and the crashing of its twelve bells is proof of its structural efficiency. Its great bell was the one Whittington heard, and Wren re-echoed the "bows" of the mediaeval tower in the clustered "consoles" which supported the final pinnacle and the great flying dragon (nine feet long) of the weather vane above.

It may be that so much work was some compensation to Wren for his private sorrows—in the autumn of 1680 his second wife died; and he never remarried.

In 1681, however, it must have given Wren the greatest satisfaction when he was elected President of the Royal Society. He no longer had time for personal experiments but he was a regular attender at meetings, a stimulating chairman and a lively critic of the Society's work. He and his friend Hooke, however, were able to discuss their joint scientific interests when they met regularly over coffee and tobacco and sometimes over dinner at City hostelries. Wren kept up his interest in scientific matters to the end of his days.

It was in this same year that Wren was able to apply himself to yet another famous skyline—that of the City of Oxford. Dr Fell—the much unloved Dean of Christ Church—wished to complete Wolsey's gateway to the front quadrangle of his college, and he asked Wren to become its architect. As when he had been consulted about Salisbury, and as when he was faced with similar stylistic problems in restoring some of the Gothic London churches, Wren did not hesitate—"I resolved it ought to be Gothick to agree with the Founder's Worke, yet I have not continued soe busy as he began". It is reported that Dr Fell at one stage wanted the gate-tower, as well as housing the great bell from Osney Abbey named "Great Tom", to function also as an observatory, and to provide for a large telescope. Wren replied that this would necessitate a flat top and not the pinnacles of the Gothic—it would have been easier "had not the parts formerly built diverted us from beginning after the better Formes of Architecture". If the observatory project was to be pursued "I feare wee shall make an unhandsome medly this way"—Wren was adamantly opposed. Yet while Wren knew which was "a better way" he never despised the Gothic as Evelyn did, and he proceeded with his own version of a Gothic clock-tower. He devised a magical combination of ogee windows, ogee window-cappings, and ogee turrets in an octagonal tower capped with an elegant ogee cupola. Tom Tower has been slightingly called Wren's "sugar-caster", but it has stood the test of time—it soars majestically over Wolsey's great unfinished quadrangle, and still worthily dominates the skyline of Oxford's dreaming spires.[19]

And this busy year saw three more of London's City churches on the way to complete restoration. St Benet, Gracechurch Street, and St Matthew's, Friday Street, were both demolished in the late nineteenth century, but at St Matthew useful rescue work was permitted—its altar piece went to Polesden Lacey House in Surrey, its font and furniture to St Clements, Fulham, and its pulpit to St Peter's Fulham. At St Mary's Abchurch, which happily survives, a tiny cobbled churchyard leads to an exquisite small masterpiece—a brick box with a charming lantern and delicate spire, and, inside a shallow painted dome roofing some of the finest carving in the City. The dome is 40 feet in diameter and rests on four plain brick walls without need of buttressing. Some of Wren's favourite craftsmen helped him here—the pulpit is by William Grey, the royal arms by William Emmett, the font by William Kempster, and the altar piece is authentic Grinling Gibbons.

Wren's fiftieth year saw the beginning of one of his major buildings for the Crown. Charles II, in spite of the opposition of his Parliament, was the first English monarch who was able to keep a standing army, and this carried with it an obligation to provide for the later welfare of men wounded and disabled in the royal service. Across the Channel, Bruant in 1670 had designed the Hôtel des Invalides for similar purposes for Louis XIV, and in 1680 J. H. Mansart had begun to build its great dome. Charles was always quick to emulate his French rival, and he sent over to France his favourite illegitimate son, the Duke of Monmouth, to borrow the drawings of the Hôtel from Louis' minister Louvois, and in due course they arrived. Meanwhile, Sir Stephen Fox, who had acquired wealth and influence as Charles' Paymaster-General, had organized a committee of management, which included both Evelyn and Wren, to build a hospital for the royal army. The position selected was the site of an old college at Chelsea which had been presented by the King to the Royal Society for its future headquarters when first chartered by Charles. It had never been used, probably because Chelsea was thought to be too far away from the centre of London for the activities of the Royal Society, and it was now sold back to the Crown. Funds were organized by Fox—he managed to extract £20,000 from the Privy Purse and an annual royal contribution of £5,000, and further funds were secured by deductions from army pay and by generous contributions from Fox himself—there was no charge on the public Exchequer. In February 1682, the King himself laid the foundation stone. It was to be Wren's first large-scale construction in brick.

The Royal Hospital Chelsea consists of three main wings set round a courtyard open towards the south and the river, with subsidiary blocks balancing the lay-out on either side. The main wings are of three equal storeys with dormers above, and the internal arrangements are surprisingly "progressive". Each inmate has his own cubicle, airy and well-lit, yet there is still ample provision for communal recreation and an open loggia outside for enjoying the sun. The central wing comprises the great hall and chapel with an imposing central vestibule dividing them, and the building materials are warm red bricks with grey Portland stone facings. Externally, the wings are accentuated by central porticos of impressive stone, Doric pillars and pilasters rising to roof-edge height, and, within, the chapel hall and council chamber are enriched by fine wood-carving and excellent plaster-work. Originally, all the windows were of the casement type; the present sash windows were inserted by Robert Adam. Above the central portico is a lantern with a cupola which some critics have considered too small. Wren wanted to re-use here one of the western towers built at St Paul's by Inigo Jones and saved from the Great Fire—it would have been some 40 feet higher than the present lantern. Unfortunately, the ecclesiastics refused to sanction the use of "sacred" stones for lay purposes.

The Royal Hospital is still a distinguished contribution to London architecture, and it is still admirably fulfilling its original function. It was not finally completed until after Charles II's death, but James II and William and Mary continued the royal patronage and it was opened for service in 1692. In the following year, Wren received a well-earned honorarium of £1,000 for his work. And, 150 years later, Thomas Carlyle, then resident in Chelsea, described Chelsea Hospital as "quiet and dignified, and the work of a gentleman" —it was a tribute which Wren himself would have understood and appreciated.[20]

In the same year that saw the Royal Hospital Chelsea begun, Wren designed what he himself considered to be his ideal parish church. In a later report, written by him in 1708, when a new Act of Parliament had been passed for the building of 50 additional London churches, he indulged in some very uncharacteristic self-praise:

I can hardly think it practicable [he wrote] to make a single Room so spacious, with Pews and Galleries, as to hold above 2,000 Persons, and all to hear the Service, and both to hear distinctly and see the Preacher. I endeavoured to effect this, in building the Parish Church of St James's, Westminster, which, I presume, is the most capacious, with these Qualifications, that hath yet been built, and yet at a solemn Time, when the Church was much crowded, I could not discern from a Gallery that 2,000 were present. In this Church I mention, though very broad, and the Middle Nave arched up, yet there are no walls of a second Order, nor Lanterns, nor Buttresses, but the whole Roof rests upon the Pillars, as doth the Galleries; I think it may be found beautiful and convenient, and, as such, the cheapest of any Form I could invent.[21]

It was shortly after the Restoration that Wren's friend and sponsor, Henry Jermyn, Earl of St Albans, had obtained authority to develop the area then known as St James's Fields, and in 1674 an excellent site (now in Piccadilly) was set aside for its parish church. Wren was appointed its architect. The exterior is plain red brick dressed with Portland stone, the square tower has a restored simple spire, and the interior is spacious and impressive. It is a galleried preaching hall with a barrel-vaulted roof supported on Corinthian pillars whose plinths rise to gallery level. The limewood reredos is a masterpiece of Grinling Gibbons—Evelyn maintained that "there was no altar anywhere in England, nor has there been any abroad, more handsomely adorned",[22] but the awkward marble font, depicting Adam and Eve standing by the Tree of Life, proves that in stone Gibbons' chisel could sometimes falter. The organ was made by Renatus Harris in 1685 for James II's Romanist chapel in the palace of Whitehall, and it was presented to St James's by Queen Mary II in 1691. Its gilded casing is also by Gibbons.

St James's was gutted by bombing in 1940 but it has been carefully and authentically restored as an accurate and worthy memorial to its architect.

St Alban's, Wood Street, also begun in this same year, was a mediaeval church which Wren restored with his customary respect for its origins—its square pinnacled Gothic tower is all that remains.

In the following year, Charles II asked Wren to design and build a new royal palace on a scale not seen before in England. The King's favourite hunting lodge at Newmarket had recently been burnt down, and he was looking for a new site with similar amenities and equally far from tiresome London Parliaments. He decided upon Winchester. There he asked for a palace which would be within easy reach of the sea and the navy for which he had a passion. Southampton Water was only twelve miles to the south, and Winchester's ancient castle, then in ruins, provided a superb position on a small hill overlooking the old capital of England and its long cathedral with the ground in front sloping gently down to the water-meadows of the Hampshire Itchen and the hall of William of Wykeham's famous school, while, westwards, good hunting terrain stretched over to Rufus' New Forest and beyond. If Louis XIV had his Versailles, Charles II would have his Winchester—and Wren became an unwitting partner in a dangerous diplomacy which at the same time sought the favour and attempted to rival the power of *Le Roi Soleil*.

In March 1683, the foundation stone for Winchester Palace was laid, and, by the time of Charles' sudden death some two

years later, the vast new palace was almost complete.[23] As at
Chelsea (and later at Greenwich) Wren's overall plans placed
the main blocks at the apex of narrowing courtyards. In their
centre was a portico of giant columns supporting a pediment
and above it a majestic dome. Two chapels were provided on
either hand with minor cupolas—one for the nominally Protestant King and the other for his devoutly Romanist Queen.
The side blocks led downhill, and a royal processional route
was planned straight from the palace entrance down to the
west door of the cathedral. This was certainly planning "for
Pompe", and it must have been one of Wren's greatest dis-
appointments—and he had many—that on Charles' death all
work ceased, and the palace was allowed to fall into decay.
Later, the buildings were adapted for use as a barracks, and
in 1894 they were finally razed in a disastrous fire. Today,
nothing remains of one of Wren's greatest buildings except
some portions of Corinthian pillars built into the modern muni-
cipal offices on the site, and some marble columns presented
to Charles by the Grand Duke of Tuscany for the great staircase which, under George I, were presented to the Duke of
Bolton and re-used at his Hackwood Park. There are no adequate original drawings of Winchester Palace surviving, but
fortunately there is an eighteenth-century engraving which
does Wren full justice. The building materials were brick with
stone facings as at Chelsea, but the roofing of the main buildings
was partly hidden by an elegant balustrading which Wren was
to use again at Hampton Court. It is sad that so magnificent
a project only survives as a memory and as a single and perhaps
not too accurate engraving.[24]

During the previous five years Wren's various projects, but
especially his responsibilities at St Paul's, had been greatly
handicapped by the political situation. In 1678 the so-called
"Popish Plot" had involved King, Parliament, Church and City
in a hysteria which gravely prejudiced progress on the new
cathedral. The infamous Titus Oates, who had invented the
"plot", had triggered off a hunting and harrying of Romanists
which the King could not stop. Charles was at loggerheads
with his Parliament and finally decided to do without one;

yet the future of the cathedral's finances depended on Parliament's renewed legislation. Furthermore, Wren's cathedral staff included one Stephen College—a master-joiner—who was also a scurrilous Protestant pamphleteer.[25] He was accused of plotting to murder the King, but a City jury refused to convict him, and only after a retrial at Oxford was he condemned and subsequently executed. The man was apparently innocent, yet Charles was persuaded to quarrel with the City on his account and even to confiscate its charter. It is not surprising that the City began to lose its enthusiasm for royal causes, and that the financial outlook for the new St Paul's now looked bad.

Nevertheless, Wren kept steadily to his overall plans, authorizing work on all sections of the site and not, as the clergy were expecting, on the choir alone. By 1685 it is true the choir and transept walls were ready up to the cornice, but the nave walls were barely to be seen above floor level, and the slow tempo may have been due to the large amount of stone-carving necessary for Corinthian capitals, swags, cherubs and rich coffering which were needed at this stage.

Meanwhile, the indefatigable Surveyor-General was given yet another responsibility. Hugh May, who had been Comptroller to Windsor Castle, died in 1684, and Wren took over the Comptrollership—it never involved him in much building, but it did mean the added work of inspection and reporting. And the restoration of City churches was still his responsibility. St Margaret Pattens in Eastcheap was built in Portland stone and had an imposing west gallery and much good woodwork. St Michael's, Crooked Lane, was demolished in 1832 to make way for new approaches to London Bridge. Its fittings were distinguished, but they were sold and have never been traced. St Andrew-by-the-Wardrobe, in Queen Victoria Street, is a simple galleried red brick church with an attractive plastered vaulting—its present interior is actually modern, although the bones of Wren's original design remain.

Wren at this stage of his long career must have been as frustrated as the Londoners were impatient—progress at St Paul's was painfully slow and its future prospects dim. It is ironic, therefore, that the sudden and unexpected death of Charles II at the early age of 54 in February of 1685 was of immediate benefit to St Paul's. Charles had been managing without a Parliament, now his brother James II was compelled to summon one to confirm his succession and ensure his revenues. The coal dues, on which St Paul's finances so largely depended, were due for renewal by Parliament—or lapsing—in two years' time; here at last was an opportunity to ensure renewal on more favourable terms. Wren promptly decided that he could do some good for his cathedral as a Member of Parliament, and he had little difficulty in getting himself elected for the Devonshire borough of Plympton St Maurice.

The prospects for St Paul's had therefore suddenly brightened after ten long years of doubt and frustration, and those same ten years had seen Wren complete some of his finest work—at Cambridge, at Oxford, at Chelsea and at Winchester—and at the same time he had been able to continue his constant task of restoring the City churches. The Surveyor-General was indeed a prodigious worker.

VIII

Politics, Palaces and Thanksgiving—1686–97

With Archbishop Tillotson and Bishop Compton in
the House of Lords and Wren himself in the House of Commons
it is not surprising that the friends of St Paul's were able to
obtain the finance they needed. The coal dues were extended
at 1/6 per chaldron to Michaelmas 1700, and not more
than one-fifth of the revenue was to go towards renovating the
City churches—the remainder was to be earmarked for St Paul's.
And, as in 1670, permission was given for reasonable borrowing.
It meant that the average income of the St Paul's fund was
increased from about £6,000 per annum to as much as £18,500
per annum or more. At a time of grave political and financial
crisis it was indeed fortunate that there was a Parliament sitting
to ensure St Paul's future—it was the only Parliament of
James II's reign. The rate for loans was fixed at six per cent, and
it proved an attractive offer—money flowed in once more,
including £1,000 from Wren in the name of his housekeeper
Miss Mary Dominick.[1] And by the end of 1687, 21 years after
the Fire of London, the last traces of Old Paul's were gone, and
the new cathedral was taking shape.

Wren's pleasure at this happy turn of events must have been
heightened by the fact that James II was anxious to do something about the Palace of Whitehall.

It was Henry VIII who first abandoned the Palace of Westminster for a new palace at Whitehall built on the site of the
London residence of the Archbishops of York. But there had
been little or no overall planning, and no great building of
distinction there until Inigo Jones built the Banqueting House
for James I. At the Restoration, between this beautiful building
and the Thames was a medley of royal lodgings and offices
crying out for demolition and planned reconstruction—it was

almost a royal slum sprawling between Jones' Renaissance masterpiece and Richard II's superb Gothic Westminster Hall, the chapel of St Stephen's and the mediaeval glories of Westminster Abbey.

There had been talk of renovation under Charles I, and Jones' able assistant John Webb had done much fruitless planning. His drawings show that he boldly suggested linking the Banqueting House with a replica which would contain a royal chapel: but nothing came of the suggestion except that, when Wren became responsible for Whitehall, the idea was revived. However, it was not until the reign of James II that actual rebuilding at last could begin.[2]

Wren was therefore heavily involved in the designing and building of a new royal chapel and a new privy gallery at Whitehall. Instead of the Portland stone of the Banqueting House, he decided to use brick with stone dressings—a speedier and less expensive method—and the chapel was of course designed for the Romanist worship of the new monarch. John Evelyn much admired Wren's work, but he was gravely shocked by the Romanism—"I could not have believed I should ever have seen such things in the King of England's Palace after it had pleased God to enlighten this nation".[3] Wren himself was less intolerant. He gave of his best to the new enterprise—his chapel was very richly decorated; Verrio painted an Assumption for its ceiling and a Salutation for its altar, and Grinling Gibbons and his partner Arnold Quellin contributed lavish carving and sculpture in wood and in stone. Within three years —on the arrival in England of the Protestant William of Orange —the chapel was stripped of its Romanist décor, and in 1691 a fire destroyed the fabric. Fortunately, before the fire, most of Wren's original altar-piece had been transferred to Hampton Court (and later to Westminster Abbey), the organ had gone to Wren's new church of St James's, Piccadilly, and two of Quellin's angels had been sent by one of the canons to the church of Burnham-on-Sea in Somerset where they can still be seen.

Wren also began for James's Queen, Mary of Modena, a pleasant lesser work at Whitehall known as Her Majesty's Privy Apartment. It included a riverside garden "curiously adorned with greens which cost some 1,000 of pounds" with a convenient covered way to river-side landing steps. The apartment had the new Dutch sash windows which had recently come into vogue, and it was in effect a typical small country house adapted for use in the corner of a great palace complex. It was completed in the next reign for Dutch William's Queen, Mary, but it was gutted by fire in 1698 and nothing now remains of it save the steps leading down to the old river-side which were revealed by excavations in very recent times.[4] Plans for major reconstruction at Whitehall of course had to be postponed until after the upheaval of the Revolution of 1688.

Meanwhile, at the other end of London's City was the fortress-palace of the Tower—another of the Surveyor-General's responsibilities. Its grim moated walls contained prison, chapels, armouries, storehouses and even a royal menagerie, and between 1685 and 1692 Wren re-designed its Great Armoury. It was a prosaic building with a simple pediment carrying the escutcheon of William of Orange, which, after fire had destroyed the rest of the building in 1841, was rebuilt into a wall on the east side of the White Tower.[5] The new armoury was not a spectacular Wren achievement—it was simply the Surveyor-General doing a routine job of work as well as it could be done.

At St Paul's there was steady if slow progress. Plans for the new west end had been finalized and were approved by King James. The two most westerly bays of the nave became one impressive entrance and assembly hall, with the chapel on the north for morning prayers and the identical chapel on the south converted into a Consistory Court and the whole was to be surmounted by a small dome. Over the north chapel there was to be a special room for the Great Model, and over the south chapel an impressive library. For the projecting west portico there are drawings which suggest that Wren contemplated a single range of colossal pillars even higher than those used by Inigo Jones for the pre-Fire restoration of Old Paul's; but the Portland quarrymen were finding difficulty in producing stones of the required dimensions. Inigo Jones' portico had pillars of some 50 feet in height, but Wren was considering pillars of some 90 feet. Finally, he decided to continue the two-storey effect of his new external walls, but added to it the greater majesty of double rows of coupled Corinthian and composite columns (of a calibre the Portland quarries could readily supply), a richly carved pediment and very much more impressive twin flanking towers—a clock tower on the south and a bell-tower on the north. The subject selected for the pediment sculpture was to be appropriately, the Conversion of St Paul.

By the spring of 1686 a start had been made with roofing the side aisles of the choir, and Wren introduced his craftsmen to the simplicity and effectiveness of saucer-dome construction. It had the advantage that its thrust was nearly vertical and therefore put less outward pressure on the walling, and its internal appearance was all of a piece with the Renaissance décor he wanted. And a lesser and hidden trouble was surmounted at this stage. The drainage system of the cathedral had over-charged the capacity of the Ludgate Hill drainage system, and Wren co-operated with the City authorities in providing adequate sewers for both the cathedral and its neighbours.

Four more City churches received Wren's advice and authority at this time. All Hallows, Lombard Street, was demolished before the Second World War, but its tower and some of its fittings and monuments were incorporated into All Hallows, Twickenham in 1940. At St Margaret, Lothbury, a plain façade and a simple lead obelisk spire belie the richness of the interior, much of it borrowed. The wide wooden screen supported by delicate double-twisted openwork wooden balusters, and the great pulpit and its sounding board came from demolished All Hallows the Great, Upper Thames Street; the communion rails, the font cover and the marble font (good enough to be attributed to Grinling Gibbons) are from demolished St Olave, Old Jewry; and the paintings of Moses and of Aaron on the richly carved reredos are from demolished St Christopher-le-Stocks, Threadneedle Street. Appropriately, it is now the church of the Bank of England over the way. Of St Mary Somerset, Upper Thames Street, only the Gothic square pinnacled tower remains—the church itself was demolished in 1871. At St Michael, Paternoster Royal, College Hill, there is little of Wren's work left except the pretty three-tiered spire which he completed in 1713. The original church held the grave of Whittington; the Wren church was badly damaged by bombing in 1944 but has been restored without its original galleries.

This steady progress in Wren's special fields was now halted by the national crisis. The deliberate Romanizing policy of the papist James II brought the monarchy into direct conflict with the English Church—and with the majority of the King's subjects. The quarrel came to a head when seven bishops were sent to the Tower and charged with seditious libel. In spite of venal judges and a packed jury, on 30 June 1688, they were all acquitted. Wren's friend Bishop Compton of London, who had previously been suspended by James, now played a prominent part in the revolution which was to overthrow the Romanist Stuart and bring the Protestant William of Orange and his wife Mary, James' elder daughter, to the English throne. Wren himself, so far as is known, took no part in the Glorious Revolution of 1688—he was preoccupied with private grief.

On the day after the acquittal of the seven bishops, Canon Holder's wife Susan—Wren's beloved sister—died and was buried in the new cathedral.

The Revolution of 1688 brought to the throne a queen with all the Stuart's love of building and respect for fine art—and both she and her husband showed a lively and sympathetic interest in London's new cathedral. They had been crowned by Bishop Compton—as staunch old Archbishop Sancroft could not reconcile himself to the new régime—and it was as a token of the new Queen's friendly encouragement that now, at the "passing of the books" at St Paul's, venison for the annual celebration dinner was provided by the Queen from her Windsor Park herds.[6]

It was as well that Wren at this period had royal support— the Whigs, who were now politically all powerful, regarded him as identified with his Tory background, and Wren for the first time in his life felt the first chill wind of opposition. He won the election for Windsor, but was unseated by Whig technical objections to the polling methods. On the other hand, the new monarchs were very much on his side. Both the King and the Queen had strong health objections to the low river-side palace of Whitehall, and much preferred the better air of Wolsey's palace at Hampton Court. Its Tudor architecture was not, however, to their liking, and Wren was immediately called in to suggest alterations and the completion of a great palace worthy of the monarchy that had defied Louis XIV.[7]

Two schemes are known to have been prepared by Wren with great speed. In the larger project, he would have retained only the Great Hall of Wolsey's palace, and a new great court-yard with a domed entrance-front and a roof-line variegated with pediments and corner pavilions, all in the best "Roman" manner, would have proclaimed William and Mary as Renais-sance and not "gothic" monarchs. Beneath the central dome was to be a great colonnaded portico in the centre of which William was to ride in triumphant effigy, while above it his escutcheon and trophies were to proclaim his ancestry and his glory. The second scheme—and no one knows why two schemes were needed and why the final scheme was what it was—was much less ambitious, but it also included a dome.

In the end, Wren found himself very much working against time—the King especially was most anxious to begin regular residence at Hampton Court. And it may be that this accounted for the fact that Wren decided to use building materials of brick with stone facings, which were readily and speedily avail-able. The Great Hall, the Clock Court and the Chapel of the old Tudor structure were retained, but new State apartments, on the north and east for the Queen and on the south for the King, were built round a new Fountain Court and on the axis of the Long Water canal (which Charles II had engineered in the park), and a new and handsome colonnading was added to the original Clock Court. The cloisters of Fountain Court bear a certain resemblance to the quadrangle front of Trinity College Library, Cambridge, and for similar reasons.

Wren wanted the flooring of the State apartments to begin from the base of the semi-circular arches which would then have carried solid carved lunettes. The King, on the other hand, felt that this made the cloister too low and too dark. In the middle of the building operations, Wren had to compromise—the flooring was to be carried on elliptical arches lower than the King wished but higher than Wren had planned. It is probable that the complication of this late alteration resulted in the collapse of part of the structure in December 1689, when two workmen were killed and several injured.

In the previous May, a new Comptroller had been forced on Wren by the new Whig politicians—one William Talman who was as much of a politician and courtier as an architect.[8] From the beginning, it was clear that the two men did not "get on", and now Talman saw his opportunity to steal a march on his superior. The King had ordered an enquiry into the accident, and Talman's report was as damaging to Wren as possible—he in fact accused him of negligence. At the enquiry, however, Wren's masons on the site spoke up for him, and Wren was exonerated—it is one of the rare occasions when anything is heard of any unpleasantness between Wren and his colleagues. It must have been a relief to Wren when on the accession of Queen Anne in 1702 Talman was eventually dismissed.

Wren's final plans for the new Hampton Court omitted his projected dome. Instead, a grandiose impression was obtained by long exterior façades of equal—and almost monotonous—height, facing the approaches to the palace from Kingston, the park and the river. In effect, these were two imposing screens giving an external illusion of grandeur, while, behind them on the new Fountain Court and the new colonnade in Clock Court, Wren lavished all the exciting detail which a great designer, supported by a superb team of great craftsmen, could produce. The round windows, for example, of Fountain Court were embroidered with stone symbolic Herculean lion skins—was not William of Orange their modern Hercules?—and "orange" wreaths deeply undercut. And within and without, the genius of the stone-carver William Emmett, of the wood-carver Grinling Gibbons, of the sculptor Cibber and of the ironsmith Jean Tijou produced an overall magnificence which had no parallel in English architecture.

On 28 December 1694, Queen Mary II unfortunately died of smallpox, and work at Hampton Court was stopped for nearly three years. It was not until 1697 that William again had the heart to concern himself with his new palace, but work was then recommenced with speed so that within a few months after the Peace of Ryswick (20 September 1697) Wren's greatest surviving palace was finished. From its park and gardens, Hampton Court gives the illusion of another Versailles. Inside,

there is a stately richness of detail which is only partially marred
by the second-rate painting of Verrio. And, today, Wren's shade
must find it galling that it is the Tudor Hall of Wolsey and its
great kitchen as much as the classical ornaments and proportions of Fountain Court which draw thousands of admirers to
the Dutch King's palace by the Thames.

Meanwhile, in London, another royal residence also needed the
Surveyor-General's attention. At Kensington, William had
bought Nottingham House, which at that time was a neat contemporary country mansion with an excellent garden in the fields
to the north-west of Westminster. In July 1689, Wren had been
ordered to enlarge Nottingham House for royal use.[9] He added
a handsome entrance court and corner pavilions on to the
Jacobean core to the west, and, later, additional wings to the
north and south. Subsequent to Wren's day, many further
alterations were to be carried out—the King's Gallery, for
example, was probably Hawksmoor's work, and the beautiful
Orangery built for Queen Anne was probably the joint work of
Hawksmoor and Vanbrugh, as also was the charming brick and
stone "alcove", or summer-house of the palace, which was later
moved to its present site at the north end of the Serpentine.
Kensington Palace was in essence a pleasant country house in
London brick with stone facings—its older parts, with pitched
roofing, dormer attics and elegant lanterned clock turret, show
Wren in pleasant if modest mood, and Dutch William found
it his most congenial town residence—in fact he was to die
there following on a fall from his horse at Hampton Court.

In February 1690 Wren received a lesser commission from
King William which he probably very much enjoyed. He was
entrusted to build an "itinerant house for His Majesty to carry
into Ireland for him to lye-in in the field; it is to be taken to
pieces and carried on two waggons that may be quickly fixt
up". It must have called forth all the ingenuity of the erstwhile
Oxford model-maker, and it is a pity that no drawing of the
royal field-headquarters has survived[10]—no doubt it was used

during the campaign which ended at the battle of the Boyne in the following July.

And several more smaller commissions were dealt with by Wren at this period. Among them it is recorded that at his old university Dean Aldrich—himself no mean architect—consulted him about the new chapel for his Trinity College. He sent Wren some designs and asked for comments, and Wren replied kindly that he had "considered the designe you sent me of your chapel which in the maine is very well, and I believe your work is too far advanced to admitt of any advice; however I have set my thoughts which will be of use to the mason to form his mouldings", and there was a payment of £2.3.0 to Wren's servant who presumably acted as messenger.

The Trinity garden quadrangle opening eastwards into the superb college garden had been originally designed by Wren in Charles II's day in two main storeys with a simple pediment and a mansard roof with dormers, but a third storey (which was added in 1802) has ruined Wren's original proportions. But Trinity's chapel, as it still is today, would certainly have been no disgrace to Wren and Grinling Gibbons, and the same can be said of the chapel and library built at this time for The Queen's College. However, the credits in the case of Trinity must rightly go to Dean Aldrich, and probably, in the case of Queen's, to Nicholas Hawksmoor.[11]

At St Paul's, the early 1690s brought both progress and problems. The most serious problem was the state of the masonry. As increasing weights were imposed on the great piers, especially in the crypt, threatening cracks appeared in some of the stone, and tell-tale oozing of mortar was visible at some of the joints. Some settlement was to be expected but not so much— the building methods Wren had criticized at Salisbury cathedral were creating similar dangers at St Paul's. The fact was that the rubble core of the great piers was sometimes shrinking and putting too great a pressure on the stone casing, and the cure, which should have been foreseen, was to lay blocks of freestone at intervals across the rubble. Meanwhile, masons had to resort to iron clamps, chains, cramps and ties—with the consequent danger of rust. And yet Wren was confident that he could surmount all the difficulties, and ultimately erect his great cupola to ride proudly and safely above the housetops. His confidence was justified in the end, but his methods in this instance ran grave and unnecessary risks.[12]

A second problem was the central space. In the Penultimate Design it was to have been dramatically lit from diagonal windows, but now such window-lighting was blocked by the heightened outer walling. Wren faced this further difficulty with his usual courage, if not with his usual success. He had to accept that the four diagonal arches of the central octagon would be less in span than the four main arches—he deliberately attempted to create the illusion that they were not. The price of that illusion—and it could not be fully convincing—was that at the four diagonal corners there would now have to be dark niches supported on somewhat odd "segmental", or non semi-circular, arches. They might suggest a set of four private "boxes" as in a theatre, but no-one has ever thought this solution an aesthetic master-stroke. But it was a solution, and no-one has ever suggested a better. It was a problem of Wren's own creation, and it must remain a mystery why he ever departed from the aisle-nave widths of the Warrant Design.

By now Wren had gathered round himself at St Paul's an excellent and experienced staff, and the machinery for controlling the vast undertaking worked reasonably smoothly. The central controlling body was a large and unwieldy Royal Commission, which at full strength included all the principal officers of state, the Bishop of London and the Dean of St Paul's. But only six members—including the Bishop and the Dean—sufficed to form a quorum.[13] Meetings of the commission were held at Guildhall once a month, and Wren was the commission's chief executive officer. His three principal assistants were now the Assistant Surveyor (until 1688 John Oliver), the Clerk of Works and Paymaster responsible for the recruitment and pay of the labour force, and a Clerk of the Cheque who seems to have been a kind of general accountant. The administrative offices were in the Convocation House over the cloisters of the old cathedral, and there Wren had his private drawing office, and a special room to house his Great Model. It is recorded that he made a regular practice of at least a weekly inspection of the works on Saturdays.[14]

It was during the rebuilding of the City churches that Wren had quickly come to recognize master-masons whom he was able to recruit to control the building of his new cathedral, and, by the time it was completed, Wren could have claimed that he had sponsored a school of masonry second to none in Europe.

His first master-mason at St Paul's was Joshua Marshall who had helped him in the building of the Monument and at several of his City churches. Unfortunately he had died prematurely in 1678, and he had been succeeded by a number of great mason-contractors who shared out the work between them. Chief among them were the brothers Thomas and Edward Strong. Thomas, who built the beautiful dome of St Stephen's Walbrook, died in 1681, but Edward was able to see St Paul's grow from foundation stone to golden cross, and he died rich and honoured in the same year as Wren—his tomb and noble monument are in St Peter's Church, St Albans. Another "foreigner", whom the Masons' Company of the City during the post-Fire emergency graciously allowed to work within the City limits, was Christopher Kempster, whose family owned quarries at Burford, Oxfordshire, and, whom, as we have seen, Wren had recommended—with excellent results—to build the "Town House" at Abingdon.[15] The master-mason responsible for the south side of the new St Paul's was Edward Pierce—the son of a painter-stainer and an all-round artist of truly astonishing virtuosity. As well as his masonry at St Paul's, his work as a wood carver at Wren's great corporation church of St Lawrence Jewry was of the highest calibre, and, if he had no other claim to fame, his marble bust of Wren would have ensured his immortality.[16] Christopher Kempster's brother William was to be responsible for the south-western tower at St Paul's—it contains the brilliantly contrived "geometrical" spiral cantilevered staircase which leads up to the cathedral library, and beneath is the charming Dean's door with stone carvings of fruits, garlands and *putti* of which Gibbons himself could have been proud. It is pleasant to know that later he was rewarded by an appreciative Wren with an additional £20 for "extraordinary Diligence and Care used in the said carving and his good performance of the same".

Each of these master-masons was also responsible for groups

of lesser masons, and all-told Wren's office had the control of a very considerable labour-force—carpenters, bricklayers, glaziers, plasterers and plumbers as well as hundreds of unskilled labourers. And now, as the basic masonry neared completion, there was a need for yet another category of skilled help—the craftsmanship of those who were to be responsible for fittings, carvings, furnishing and decoration. Here, again, Wren was able to call upon and inspire a group of artist-craftsmen of exceptional ability.

The most famous of these men was, of course, Grinling Gibbons,[17] whom Wren had first used at Trinity College, Cambridge, and later at the churches of St Mary Abchurch and St James's, Piccadilly. Now Wren was able to offer his talent its fullest scope at St Paul's. Gibbons' woodcarving was clearly inspired by the great Dutch flower-painters, and no one has ever surpassed his skill in carving swags of flowers, fruits and seed-pods of astonishing realism in the sober material of natural woods. On the other hand, his figure work never equalled his decorative work, and his celebrated *putti* at St Paul's scarcely deserve their fame. It is now believed that some of his best work, other than in wood, was in fact the work of the Dutchman Arnold Quellin, who became his partner about 1680.[18] Nevertheless, Gibbons' stone bas-reliefs on the south walls of St Paul's and on the spandrels of the piers of the central dome, and his superb wood-carving on the chancel choir-stalls, the Bishop's throne, the Lord Mayor's seat, the carved screens facing the aisles and the organ casing illustrate his genius at its very considerable best.

A close rival to Gibbons was Jonathan Maine, whose work can still be admired on the exteriors of St Paul's western chapels, on the superb interior wooden screen of what is now the Chapel of St Michael and St George, and on the roof and furniture of the cathedral's library.[19] And two lesser sculptors were also to make their contributions—Caius Gabriel Cibber, and Francis Bird. Cibber's work at St Paul's can be seen at its best in the eight richly carved keystones to the great arches of the central space beneath the dome, and in the symbolic phoenix above the significant word *Resurgam* on the exterior pediment of the south transept.[20] Bird was a much younger man who had trained in Italy—he was to be used by Wren for the carving on the tomb of his daughter Jane, for the statue of Queen Anne outside the west-front, for figures on the parapet above the west door and for the relief sculpture depicting the Conversion of St. Paul in the western pediment.[21]

And there was yet another distinguished immigrant who was to owe his fame and fortune to Wren—Jean Tijou, the Huguenot exile, whom he used for structural and decorative metal-work both at St Paul's and at Hampton Court. It was Tijou who was to construct the great iron chain which binds the base of the central dome at St Paul's, and who produced the great gilded wrought-iron gates (and the several lesser grilles) in the choir which are perhaps the most splendid works of art in the interior of St Paul's.[22]

The question arises as to how Wren and his masons and his artist-craftsmen actually worked. Where stone relief-work was required, there must have been agreement at the design stage as to where a sculptor's chisel was needed—stone carving could not merely be "applied". Where wood-carving and metal-work were concerned, again, the Surveyor's controlling voice must have decreed where they were needed, and to a certain degree outlined theme and scale. There is no evidence that in such matters Wren ever had any serious difficulty with his staff, and there is evidence that he was the first to appreciate their potential skills and to offer them the fullest scope. Wren was perhaps fortunate in his personal assistant on the design side, Nicholas Hawksmoor[23] a pupil with a genuine reverence for his master. It was not the least of Wren's virtues that he was able to keep his band of touchy geniuses in reasonably happy co-operation over a long span of difficult years—the only exception being a later dispute over remuneration with Edward Pierce.[24]

From 1693 to the end of 1697 Wren's chief objective was to complete the choir of St Paul's so that it could be used for services while not neglecting the rest of the structure; he seems to have had a shrewd suspicion that his complete plans might be thwarted by a decision—for economy reasons—to remain content with only a finished choir. He would indeed finish the choir, but he had no intention of abandoning his cupola, his central space, his transepts and his magnificent entrance portico.

The roofing of the choir, therefore, was urgent, but John Langland, Wren's master-carpenter, was finding it more and more difficult to obtain oak of the required calibre. However, in 1693, the wealthy Duke of Newcastle had heard of the trouble and had very generously offered the authorities 50 great oaks free of charge[25] from his Welbeck estates, and during the next two years enough huge oak timbers were transported by road to Bawtry and thence by river to Hull, and so by sea to London, to provide for both choir and nave. The massive tie-beams needed oak timber over 40 feet long, and iron was used for strengthening and bracing throughout the king-posted structure. In the construction of the shallow saucer-domed vaulting underneath, Wren was able to put into practice what he had long preached in theory—the covering of a brick core with his special "Roman" plaster. It was a mixture of fine sand and cockleshell lime which depended for its efficiency on the great length of time devoted to its pounding. Wren maintained—and he was proved correct—that it set as hard and as durable as stone.[26]

In October 1693, Wren submitted to the commissioners his complete scheme for the internal fittings of the choir—and they were accepted. There is evidence that Wren would have preferred to have done without the traditional choir screen, and he actually designed a high altar beneath an impressive pillared *baldachino*, but he was overruled by the conservative clergy and therefore made plans for a choir screen to be surmounted by the great organ. For the decorative carving of all the woodwork he was happy to commission Grinling Gibbons, and under Wren's controlling hand the great craftsman worked for nearly three years in the chancel of the cathedral. At the same time Jean Tijou was given the contract for the wrought-iron gates in the inner chancel and for the iron-work for the great windows.

The authorities were determined that the new cathedral's organ would be an instrument worthy of the great scale of the rest of the project. They took the advice of Dr John Blow, the distinguished composer who was organist to Westminster Abbey, in choosing its designer. There were two obvious candidates—the German Bernard Schmidt, known familiarly as "Father Smith", and the Frenchman Renatus Harris. Smith

had built the organs for the Abbey, Durham Cathedral, St
Margaret's, Westminster, and some of the new City churches,
and Harris too could refer to many important clients. The
commission eventually went to Smith, probably because he
was a Protestant whereas Harris was a papist. The contract
with Smith was made in December 1694, and he was provided
with a special workshop and metal-forge near the west end of
the north choir aisle. The organ's casing, however, was not
Smith's responsibility—it was to be decorated with some of
the finest wood-carving of Grinling Gibbons.[27]

It must be remembered that at this stage the chancel of
St Paul's was primarily to be self-contained and all-sufficient
for great State occasions when a large and distinguished con-
gregation would be present. Behind the choir stalls and on
either side of the organ Wren therefore provided public galleries
in two tiers. And for a cathedral which was eventually to provide for ordinary services as well—with usually small congrega-
tions—Wren had the boldness to insist on a pulpit which could
be moved to the best strategic position for each occasion. He
designed a pulpit on wheels of which Grinling Gibbons was
again the distinguished decorator.[28]

In 1860 Smith's organ was divided and sited on either side
of the choir so that an uninterrupted vista was obtained from
the west doors, over the crossing, and beyond to the high altar
at the far east end. The Victorians built a pink marble reredos
and altar in 1888 which remained in all its ugliness until
destroyed by the bombing of 1941. Today, the vista remains but
a spectacular *baldachino*, based on the relics of a surviving model
of Wren's at the cathedral, is its worthy culmination. The long
vista is impressive, but there are critics who suggest that it
takes away from the importance of Wren's central space.[29]

The great concentration of craftsmanship in the chancel area
of St Paul's had not meant a halt to progress on the rest of the
structure. By the end of 1695, the outer walls of nave chapels,
western towers and west front were completed to the height of
the first cornice, and the great arches which were eventually to
support the central dome were only needing the embellishment
of their great keystones—some seven feet high and five feet

broad. Wren turned to Cibber, whom he had used on the Monument and at Hampton Court, for this important task— and Cibber responded by some of his most impressive carving.

Although the design of Wren's central dome and western towers were still to be finally determined there seemed a reasonable prospect that he would see his *magnum opus* through to a finish. But Wren's optimism now received two serious setbacks. In February 1696, news arrived of a serious disaster at Portland, and at about the same time the finances of the whole project seemed to be in mortal danger. At the Portland quarries, a landslide necessitated a new roadway and new harbour works, and the situation seemed so serious that in the following spring Wren himself, Edward Strong and Nicholas Hawksmoor took the long coach-journey to Dorset to speed repairs and obtain greater co-operation from the frequently obstinate and awkward quarrymen.[30] Their journey was successful.

But the cathedral's finances were an even greater worry. The costs of finishing the choir were mounting, and the country's financial situation, owing to the war with France, meant that borrowing was neither easy nor cheap. In addition, many of the masons and craftsmen were owed money for fees and work. It was probably at Wren's suggestion that some relief was obtained by the creditor employees allowing what they were owed to be regarded as loans repayable at six per cent interest— Wren himself contributing £1,000 in his own name. But the final relief could only come from parliamentary finance.

It was estimated that at least £178,285 would be needed to complete St Paul's fabric, and the commissioners petitioned Parliament to renew the coal-dues rate at 12d per chaldron for a further period of twelve years after 1700. A deputation of members came to inspect the works at St Paul's, and as a result they expressed their dissatisfaction at the slowness of progress but agreed that, unless the whole building could be finished, colossal expenditure would be wasted, and that further finance was necessary. Wren's policy of refusing to build in sections had paid off—in March 1697, a coal duty of 12d per chaldron was granted for a further sixteen years after 1700, but one-fifth of the proceeds were earmarked for the City churches, one-sixth for Westminster Abbey and £3,000 for St Thomas's Hospital, and only the remainder was to go to St Paul's. Moreover, in an incredible spirit of mean exasperation, the Commons insisted that, until the cathedral was finished, the Surveyor was to receive only half his salary "therebye the better to encourage him to finish . . . with the utmost Diligence and Expedition".[31] It was an egregious insult to the man on whom all the responsibility rested and who had suffered most from difficulties beyond his control. A lesser man might at this stage have thrown in his hand. But Wren, now in his late sixties, was determined to see his masterpiece through to the finish without alteration from other designers. His only sign of pique was that, after two years on his half pay, he sent in a bill for petty disbursements in the service of St Paul's over the previous twenty-five years for the paltry sum of £200. And it must have gladdened Wren's heart that one of his oldest friends, Thomas Sprat, now Dean of Westminster, had promptly appointed him Surveyor to the Abbey at the £100 per annum of which Parliament had deprived him. Wren swallowed his pride, and proceeded to finish St Paul's chancel.

In September of this same year (1697) William III concluded the Peace of Ryswick by which the great Louis XIV of France was compelled to recognize "the little Lord of Breda" as the rightful King of England, and England as the equal of France among the great powers of Europe. Here was the right occasion for a Celebration Opening to the choir of the new St Paul's— and all preparations were speeded up to prepare for the magnificent thanksgiving service which was to be held in the completed choir on 2 December 1697. Cleaning, painting "marbling", colourful furnishings and regal tapestries did full justice to an east end which John Evelyn described as "certainly a piece of Architecture without reproach". Wren's friend Bishop Compton preached to the text of "I was glad when they said unto me let us go into the House of the Lord" before a very distinguished company. Wren could have felt that at last his major work was appreciated.

IX

Evening—1698-1711

IN HIS LATE sixties and early seventies, Wren added to all his
other responsibilities two major projects for royal palaces—one
at Greenwich, which was finally carried out and exists today,
the other at Whitehall, which remains a masterpiece only on
paper.

Some five miles down river from London Bridge is the
village of Greenwich. There the Tudors had built a palace
which, by Wren's day, had fallen into decay, and on a small
hill above it, Inigo Jones had built his famous Queen's House.
Under Charles II it had been decided to renovate the decaying
fabric of the palace, and one block of a new palace had been
actually completed by John Webb—the so-called King Charles'
block close to the river. It was a dignified and simple design
with a central pedimented portico and pavilion ends faced
with giant Corinthian pillars to the full height of the roof.
Further developments had been thwarted by Charles' chronic
financial difficulties, and John Evelyn's grandiose plans for the
palace gardens had come to nothing for the same reason.

James II, who was a keen sailor and had seen active naval
service against the Dutch, decided that Greenwich—close to
the naval dockyards at Deptford—was an ideal location for a
hospital for seamen to balance the provision made at Chelsea
by his brother for England's soldiers. His reign was too short
and too troubled for anything to mature, but in the following
reign Queen Mary II, after the Anglo-Dutch naval victory
over the French off La Hogue in May 1692, had decreed that
the hospital should be built as a thank-offering. In 1694 she
had issued her royal charter of confirmation, and an advisory
commission had been formed; and "the Surveyor, nominated
a Director and Chief Architect of this great Undertaking, he

cheerfully engag'd in the work, gratis". Wren's difficult task
had been to continue from where John Webb had left off.

Wren's first scheme for a new Greenwich Hospital had been
to build a counterpart to Webb's block on the east side of a
large open courtyard facing the river. This was to lead into a
narrower courtyard flanked by dormitories and culminate in
a semi-circular colonnade, in the centre of which was to be
a great pedimented portico leading to the main block of the
hospital containing a hall and a chapel and surmounted by
a single impressive dome. It was a plan which had affinities
with his design for Winchester Palace, but there was a difficulty
—it would have completely screened The Queen's House from
the river front, and Queen Mary had therefore rejected it.
After the Queen's death, William of Orange had in loyalty
continued her ban, and Wren had been compelled to think
again.

His revised scheme, which William accepted, was in essence
the Greenwich which has survived, although of course, there
have been many later additions. The great courtyard of the
first scheme was retained but the remaining buildings were
grouped so as to reveal The Queen's House at the centre of
the lay-out but at the farthest point from the river front.
Halfway back, and framing the distant view of Inigo Jones'
masterpiece, was on the west the great hall and on the east
the chapel, each surmounted by lofty identical domes on high
drums. Work had begun in 1696, and the hall and chapel
had been begun two years later. From 1702 onwards, when
John Vanbrugh became Comptroller of the Works, Wren himself—he was now in his seventies—had little to do with the
actual construction, but Vanbrugh and Hawksmoor, and later
Thomas Ripley, faithfully carried out his master-plans.[1]

Greenwich Hospital—now the Royal Naval College—has been
ranked among the masterpieces of English architecture, but it has
one fatal flaw. It was designed deliberately to frame The Queen's
House—a building only two storeys high and therefore bound
to be dwarfed by Wren's great domes; and the whole lay-out
is only satisfactory when seen in a bird's eye view or, to a
lesser degree, when viewed from across the river, where in
Wren's day were open fields and where today is a sprawl of
very congested industrial development. Nevertheless, Wren's

twin domes still dominate the lower reaches of the Thames, and his Painted Hall—the artist was Sir James Thornhill—is probably the most lavish and magnificent of all English interiors.

In 1698, a disastrous fire swept through Whitehall Palace. King William was not personally interested in Whitehall—he suffered badly from asthma and therefore preferred Hampton Court and Kensington. Nevertheless, he felt it his duty to see that England's central palace was suitably rebuilt, and Wren must have felt very much as he had felt after London's Great Fire—here was a superb opportunity for designing on the grand scale. William commissioned him to prepare designs for a new Whitehall, and Wren with his usual speed produced two for the King's consideration. Both were majestic and impressive—neither was ever carried out.

When the fire struck, Wren—his official residence was not far away at Scotland Yard—was foremost in helping to save the Banqueting House from the flames.[2] It is not, therefore, surprising that in both his Whitehall schemes he made Jones' building the centre-piece. But Wren's respect for the Old Master did not preclude him from boldly suggesting alterations and additions to his work which Jones himself might have deplored. In his first scheme, he added a colossal portico to the middle of the side elevation making it the main entrance, and on either hand he added—it was inevitable—domed staircase towers. In his second scheme, he reverted to Webb's original plan and proposed duplicated Banqueting Houses on either side of a central portico of great magnificence adorned with statuary, and including an equestrian statue of King William himself. But neither scheme was ever begun, and no one for certain knows why. Both schemes would have involved the replanning not only of old Whitehall, but of the whole Westminster area as well, including the Abbey, the Parliament Houses and Westminster Hall. Yet Wren's conception—the drawings have only recently come to light—shows him in his mature majestic prime, and, even if some of them are clearly the work of his assistants, there is no mistaking the overall scale of a master of what has come to be known as "English baroque". Wren's great Whitehall Palace complex only exists on paper, but it is nevertheless a significant witness to his genius, and for lack of its realization the English monarchy has had to remain content with the tiny Tudor palace of St James's until, in late Georgian and Edwardian times, it converted a nobleman's undistinguished house into an undistinguished palace turning its back on the royal Mall.

And now a lesser fire, but with possible consequences too fearful to contemplate, halted progress at St Paul's. On 27 February 1699, horrified workmen noticed that Father Smith's organ-pipe forge, just outside the north-east vestry, was on fire. The blaze was dangerously close to the new choir screen, and before it was under control the north choir aisle was a disheartening sight—cracked and stained masonry, broken marble paving and dirt and ashes everywhere. The main fabric, however, was saved, but the extent of the crisis can be gauged by the fact that the necessary repairs took two years to complete.[3] The new St Paul's had a very narrow escape from total destruction, and immediate and more stringent safety precautions were enforced throughout the cathedral site.

The next step was the completion of the transepts, and in particular the insertion of large semi-circular panels in bas-relief inset into the pediments. The one for the north transept was entrusted to Grinling Gibbons, the one for the south transept to Cibber. Gibbons' heraldic composition was finished first, and it was a disappointment—Gibbons was never really happy with stone as his medium. For the south pediment Wren took greater precautions. Cibber's first design was "mocked up" in board and hoisted into position so that Wren could judge the effect. He was not satisfied, and Cibber tried again. His second design showed a phoenix rising from flames surmounting the significant word *Resurgam*, which Wren had found such an encouraging omen twenty-five years before. It seemed appropriate and it was accepted—it was Cibber's last and perhaps most impressive work—he died shortly after its completion.[4]

As the new century began, financial embarrassment again

delayed progress. Revenue would now be little more than a third of what it had been, and work had to be slowed down. But once again politics did Wren a good turn. There was a prospect of a Tory revival, and the Tories were traditionally the friends of St Paul's. If the Tories achieved power, therefore, the Coal Dues Act might be revised in the cathedral's favour. Wren seems to have hoped to overcome his difficulties in two ways—by propaganda and by himself again becoming a Member of Parliament.

Since the publication of the Warrant Design, Wren had been keeping his own counsel with reference to the central dome and the western towers. There is evidence in many undated drawings that he was constantly experimenting, examining precedents in engravings, and making model after model; but he had reached no definite conclusions. On the other hand, the public were now entitled to know that neither the Warrant Design's cupola and spire nor the Great Model's dome was to dominate their capital. Wren authorized, with the commission's permission, the engraving of various views of his new conceptions. Jan Kip, a celebrated Dutch engraver, drew an exterior prospect from the north. Simon Gribelin, a Frenchmen, engraved the west front. And later Robert Trevitt—a fine English engraver—published views of both the projected exterior and interior. The great central dome shown in these engravings derived from Michelangelo's and Bramante's schemes for the dome of St Peter's, and the western towers were still based on the Bramante *Tempietto*—in fact they were all misleading, and Wren himself was still not sure of his final designs. All these very fine engravings were distributed to persons of influence, and of course were available in the print-shops—they were an early instance of the very modern practice of what is now called public relations.[5]

Wren's second line of attack was again to take a hand in politics. In September 1701, the exiled King James II died, and Louis XIV, contrary to the treaty of Ryswick, recognized his son as King of England. William III was naturally outraged, and England prepared to renew the war against France. A new Parliament was summoned for December, and Wren became a Member for the borough of Weymouth with Melcombe Regis. But in the New Year it was clear that the King was seriously ill, and on 8 March 1702, he died. Once again a royal death meant good fortune for Wren. Princess Anne— the second daughter of James II—ascended the throne. She was a member of the Tory purple, an ardent supporter of the Church of England, and a good friend of St Paul's and Sir Christopher Wren. In the new Parliament, the Tories were soon in power and the financial difficulties of St Paul's were quickly and handsomely settled—this time there had been no need for Wren to seek membership. The coal duty was raised by as much as two shillings a chaldron for eight years from May 1708—Wren could feel that at least his greatest creation would be finished one day even if he himself did not see it. He was now in his seventies.

On 12 November 1702, St Paul's saw another great thanks-giving service, this time in honour of the new monarch who was present. Not long afterwards, a very much simpler and sadder ceremony took place in St Paul's crypt—Wren's be-loved daughter Jane was buried there near the graves of Canon and Mrs Holder, and later Francis Bird was com-missioned to carve on her tombstone a bas-relief of St Cecilia at the organ and a Latin inscription which read "like her father fond of learning, dutiful, kind, home-loving, an expert musician". Wren's old age was full of private sorrows.

The new reign involved of course a new commission for St Paul's, and there was change too at the Office of Works. Talman was deprived of his post as Comptroller in favour of John Vanbrugh—soldier, playwright, wit and soon a great architect with a great respect for Wren. It meant that Wren could begin to shed some of his burdens onto the shoulders of his juniors—and in particular it meant that he was less concerned with the complicated responsibility for Greenwich Hospital.

At St Paul's there was all the excitement of adding the final touches. Expenditure rose from about £14,000 in 1702–3 to nearly £37,500 in 1706–7, and loans at six per cent flowed in —Wren's own contribution reached £1,900. The central space was finished up to what is now known as the Whispering Gallery, whose graceful railing was the work of Jean Tijou. For the north-west tower, Wren had been able to secure a very famous old bell which had stood near Westminster Hall for centuries—it was called "Edward of Westminster" because it had been cast in the reign of Edward III. It weighed four tons, and had been installed in a temporary position at St Paul's on New Year's Day of 1699. Sightseers had been allowed to inspect it (and so provide a little extra revenue for the Building Fund) and this may have caused the crack which later necessitated a complete recasting with added new metal.[6] For the south-west tower, Wren commissioned a clock from a distinguished London clock-maker named Langley Bradley —its mechanism was something of an achievement as the minute-hand had to be seven feet long.[7] It was therefore high time that Wren settled once and for all the design for the upper parts of the western towers. He decided to abandon the "tempietto" effects of the Warrant Design, and instead he produced the baroque steeples which are among his greater creations. Mouldings, cornices, Corinthian pillars, consoles, urns and tiny cupolas are all embroidered together in a happy exuberance, and of course surmounted by the symbolic gilded copper pineapples of contemporary fashion. The north-west tower owed its metal work to Tijou, the south-west tower to the work of a very expert female coppersmith, Jane Brewer.[8]

And now, at last, the architect had to determine once and for all the details of that central cupola which had been at the summit of his dreams for so long. At some time between 1703 and 1706, the design of the great dome of St Paul's was at last settled, after a gestation period of some 25 years.

It was a *sine qua non* that St Paul's dome should dominate the London sky-line and yet Wren was determined on a stone lantern which could be seen from near as well as far. He therefore ruled out a semi-circular dome in favour of an ovoid which was to ride high over an attic storey and rest securely on a massive stone drum supported by Corinthian pillars and buttressed by solid masonry niches. The top of the cross he planned above the lantern was to be 366 feet from ground level.

Internally, complications immediately began. First, an internal, much shallower dome was required to bring so dizzy a height within the comfortable scale of those standing in the central space below. Wren decided to leave a dramatic open "eye" in this dome—the Romans had done the same at the

Pantheon—to afford a glimpse, but only a glimpse, of the greater height above, and it was to be lit by windows hidden behind the open columns of the great outer drum, and some extra light was also to be shed down through the "eye". How was this latter effect to be obtained? By a stratagem which was Wren's greatest stroke of magic.

Between the shallow inner dome and the outer visible ovoid dome, he decided to insert yet another structure—an invisible cone of brick to carry the weight of the great stone lantern. At the top of this brick cone were to be eight openings through which light could stream down from invisible windows immediately below the lantern.[9]

It was a brilliant conception. Wren may have been studying the oast houses of Kent, he may have seen engravings of a similar effect in the Baptistery at Pisa, he had used internal cones to stabilize several of his finest City steeples, but broadly his hidden brick cone at St Paul's was to be without parallel or precedent, and once again purists have accused him of illegal "shamming".[10] As far as the Surveyor was concerned, his cone was to be a logical answer to a very difficult practical problem, and its "unorthodoxy" was of no relevance. Work began forthwith.

Meanwhile, Wren's master-masons—and no lesser craftsmen —had been entrusted with the repairs which the settling and cracking of the great supporting piers had necessitated. They had the delicate task of "opening the Joynts of the Leggs of the Dome" to stabilize the masonry's rubble core, and the building accounts prove that at intervals from 1691 until 1716 such repair works, of great technical difficulty and of some magnitude and of vital importance, cost well over £7,500.[11] In constructing the drum for the dome Wren had already incorporated an iron chain of great strength to prevent spreading, and in February 1707 what is known as the "Great Chain" was wrought by Tijou to bind the structure at the point where outer and inner dome and cone conjoined, and in November of the same year more chains were inserted in the crown of the outer dome. In recent times, further security work has been found necessary, and in 1928–9 stainless steel was called in aid. In Wren's defence, it must be remembered that his technical equipment was primitive compared with the electronic devices of modern structural engineers, and Wren's ghost must have been delighted with the praise that modern renovators have always joined with their critical comments. To balance a lantern weighing 850 tons over a dome 350 feet above London was no easy accomplishment.[12]

With this stone lantern Wren took exceptional pains. It was "mocked up", first in models, then full size on the ground, and each stone was cut and dressed ready to be hauled into place without further attention. Its mason was the son of Edward Strong, who had been the young Christopher Wren's travelling companion in Europe. And in May 1708, Francis Bird signed a contract for preparing first a model and then the actual ball and cross which would ride above the lantern. They were to be of gilded copper—the ball was to be six feet in diameter and the arm of the cross was to be almost thirteen feet in span. It was a formidable task well executed by Bird and his metal-founder Andrew Niblett.[13]

It was about this time that Wren began to find himself in public discord with the St Paul's commissioners. The first sign that this relationship had turned sour had come in 1707, when a dispute arose as to the roofing material for the outer dome. Wren had wanted and prescribed lead, but the commissioners were being "lobbied" by the very active English copper industry, and the Commons in fact authorized copper. Fortunately, Wren had already gone ahead, and leading was well under way. The House of Lords rejected the Commons recommendation, and the dispute ended—except that gilded copper was used for the cross and ball and for the finials of the two western towers, and to this Wren had had no objection.[14]

Two years later, a second dispute arose concerning the railings which Wren had planned to surround the whole cathedral site. Wren wanted wrought-iron, but he was overruled and compelled to accept the cast-iron railings of one Richard Jones.[15] Wren suspected jobbery, but in fairness to Jones it must be recorded that, whatever the financial arrangements may have been, his cast iron—coming from the ancient iron foundries of Lamberhurst in Kent—was of excellent quality, and portions still survive.

A third and longer-lasting dispute also began in 1709, when the question first arose as to how the interior of the inner

visible dome was to be decorated. It is believed that Wren
had intended either mosaic-work or coffering on the lines of
his dome at St Stephen's Walbrook in the City. The commissioners desired mural paintings, and they organized a kind
of closed competition from which the Italian Pellegrini and
the English James Thornhill emerged as the most successful
contestants.[16] They were both asked to submit further cartoons
on specially prepared models, and, as was to be expected, the
work of the Englishman was preferred. The dispute continued
for several years, and it was not until June 1715 that after
much wrangling the commission gave Thornhill the order to
proceed. Thornhill's work in the Painted Hall at Greenwich is
justly famed, but his work on St Paul's inner dome was in some
ways a disaster, and certainly not to the liking of Wren. Tech-
nically, Thornhill's work was an achievement, but his *trompe
l'oeil* arches are at war with the lines of Wren's dome, and
exaggerate a height which Wren was anxious to diminish in
effect. Wren had once more been overruled.

But, in the meantime, Wren had had his days of triumph.
In his relationships with four monarchs there was never anything but cordiality and appreciation—it was only when the
House of Hanover arrived that Wren failed to find royal
favour. He had even been on dining terms with the Cromwells.
Charles II had treasured his craftsmanship and given him his
knighthood. He had received handsome presents from Queen
Mary II, and now Queen Anne tokened her friendship with
a superb watch (it survives at the Soane Museum) and a
beautiful bureau. Her reign had been begun with the thanks-
giving service of 1702—it was only the first of several, the
most important of which was the celebration on 7 September
1704 for Marlborough's victory at Blenheim when the Queen
"full of jewels" was accompanied by the Duchess of Marlborough "in a very plain gown" at the magnificent State ceremony in the new St Paul's.[17]

And at last in October 1708, a much simpler but more
satisfying ceremony took place. Thirty-three years before, the
foundation stone of St Paul's had been laid without ceremony.
Now, the last stone was added to the lantern by Wren's elder
son, born in the year the new cathedral was begun, and
assisted by the master-mason Edward Strong whose brother

had helped to lay the foundation stone. There is some doubt
as to the exact date, but it may well have been 20 October,
the Surveyor's seventy-sixth birthday. And there is a tradition
that Wren himself was able to witness the very simple ceremony
from the basket slung from a giant crane which he used for
inspecting progress—he was the sole survivor of those who had
witnessed the laying of the foundation stone.[18]

As London's new cathedral was revealed in all its glory to the
expectant citizens, the skyline of the city was already punc-
tuated by Wren's galaxy of spires, towers and steeples. If they
are considered in stylistically similar groups it is astounding how
much variety Wren was able to achieve within each group,
and to have produced 52 church towers each of which has
some feature, or sometimes many features, of originality is not
the least of Wren's claims to fame.

Of the simpler square brick towers, often with stone facings,
St Clement Eastcheap remains a good sample—it had been
finished in 1687. But most of Wren's towers date from the
early 1700s when the City Fathers felt that they could afford
them. Typical of these is the Gothic pinnacled square tower
of St Mary Aldermary which was completed in 1704. Of the
onion-spired variety, St Peter's, Cornhill and St Mary Abchurch are charming examples—they had been completed by
1686. Of the Gothic spire style, St Margaret Pattens (1687) is
perhaps the most impressive. But Wren's truly baroque creations, with one exception, all belong to the early 1700s—the
exception was St Mary-le-Bow completed as early as 1680.
The steeples of St Bride's, Fleet Street (1701–3), of Christ
Church, Newgate Street (1704), of St Magnus Martyr, Lower
Thames Street (1705) and the two western towers of St Paul's
(1705–6) show, in constructional ingenuity and in their richness
and originality of detailing, Wren in mature perfection. Even
if there can be reservations about the "wedding-cake" effect
of St Bride's, there is no dispute about the quality of the remainder.[19] No other architect and no other city can equal in
quality and in quantity the work of Wren for the City of
London, and it is fortunate that the 28 surviving Wren churches

and the five solitary Wren steeples include most of his best work.

Early in the year 1711, Wren asked the commissioners that, as St Paul's was completed except for some internal details, he might receive the arrears of salary due to him. The commissioners referred the matter to Parliament, and once again politics came to the Surveyor's aid. The Tories were back in power, and Wren's petition was therefore favourably received —it was decreed that he should be paid arrears of £1,425 at or before Christmas 1711.[20] Wren's critics on the commission —Dr Godolphin, the new Whig Dean, and Dr Francis Hare, Chaplain-General to the Duke of Marlborough—were affronted, and a sustained campaign was begun to discredit the Surveyor, and if necessary drive him from office. As a first move, Richard Jennings, master-carpenter at St Paul's and a firm supporter of Wren, was accused of various financial malpractices and dismissed without reference to the Surveyor.[21] Court proceedings against Jennings were started, but the Attorney-General ruled that there was insufficient evidence and they were abandoned. Jennings' successor was John James, a surveyor, and he was given the same salary as Wren—£200. It was a very unhappy state of affairs. The churchyard still remained to be cleared, and its fencing was incomplete. In front of the western portico, Francis Bird's statue of Queen Anne with its attendant symbolic maidens representing Great Britain, Ireland, France and America was still hidden behind its hoarding. Inside, the dome was shrouded in scaffolding awaiting the selected painter. For the chapter house, which was being built to the north of the site, Wren was still using Jennings, and there were further squabbles with Dr Hare about its fittings. The final chapter in the history of the construction and decoration of the new St Paul's was a sordid anti-climax.

X

Sunset—1711–23

WREN WAS NOW approaching 80 years of age. His cathedral
was finished except for certain fittings and details. He had been
able to shed the burden of Greenwich Hospital without sacri-
ficing his design authority. But he was still Surveyor-General,
and he was still Surveyor to Westminster Abbey, and he had no
intention of relinquishing either of these major responsibilities.
Perhaps he would have been well advised to retire gracefully
from active service at this late stage, but the simple fact is that
he could not recognize any diminution in his abilities and saw
no reason why he should give way to lesser men. But the affair
of Jennings had showed that, even though the creative artist
was still indefatigable, the administrator was possibly slackening
his grip on the routine of his office. And there was worse to
come.

In April 1712, a 42-page pamphlet appeared entitled *Frauds
and Abuses at St Paul's,* and there is no doubt that its author,
who remained anonymous, was in fact Wren's commissioner
critic, Dr Hare. It was a malicious attack on Wren's conduct
of affairs at St Paul's and accused him, his assistants and his
chief artificers of dishonesty, and even of fraudulent dealings.
Three answering pamphlets were published in the following
year in which Wren's associates defended themselves with
statistics, affidavits and unfortunately with unpleasant counter-
accusations. Whether Wren himself wrote any of these pamphlets is doubtful but it is certain that he was well aware of
them, and must share responsibility for their virulence. It is
an episode which does no participant any credit, and which
resulted in nothing more than increased ill-feeling amongst
those responsible for the completion of St Paul's.[1] It may be
that Wren himself was missing the helpful advice of old friends

—Hooke had died in 1708, Evelyn had died in 1706, and both
Bishop Compton and Bishop Sprat died in 1713—his old age
was lonely.

But Wren had had very happy relationships with Sprat at
Westminster Abbey, and, just before his old friend died, he was
able to complete a report on that ancient fabric which was a
remarkable composition for a man of 81. As in his report on
Salisbury Cathedral, while criticizing the old builders he nevertheless refused "to deviate from the old Form which would be
to run into a disagreeable Mixture which no Person of good
Taste could relish". When John Evelyn had described Henry
VII's chapel at the abbey he had not minced his words—he
had the greatest contempt for "crincle-crancle". When Wren
considered it, he was more tolerant, and thought it "a nice
embroidered work"—he had a genuine regard for the Gothic
builders. He proffered detailed drawings for the restoration of
the abbey's north transept; they were actually drawn by his
assistant William Dickinson but approved and signed with his
own trembling signature, and they show a touching loyalty to
the old Gothic idiom. He staunchly advocated the addition of
a central spire and two western towers. A spire at the crossing,
he reported, will "add a proper Grace to the whole Fabrick
and the West end of the City which seems to want it"—it was a
judgement which is still relevant. In the end, there was to be
no central spire, and the western towers were left to the young
Hawksmoor in one of his less inspired moods.[2] Wren's devotion
to Westminster Abbey at so great an age is remarkable and
praiseworthy in a man who had been responsible for a cathedral
which in so many ways, but not in every way, was the perfect
antithesis to the abbey's "Gothick".

On 7 July 1713, Wren attended his last thanksgiving service
at St Paul's—it was in celebration of the Treaty of Utrecht.
Unfortunately, Queen Anne was too ill to be present, but the
huge concourse was able to admire the newly unveiled statue
of the Queen in robes of state with her attendant symbolic
maidens executed in marble, and in pride of place facing the
western portico. Incidentally its railings were of wrought-iron
—the last work at St Paul's of Jean Tijou.

In the following year Queen Anne died. In the unreliable
chronology of Wren's life and work which appears in *Parentalia*

there is a revealing entry in Greek: "And there arose a king that knew not Joseph, and Gallio cared for none of these things."[3] The end of Wren's professional career was near—the accession of the Hanoverian George I soon involved great changes at the Office of Works. The office of Surveyor was put into commission with Wren still a member and still entitled Surveyor-General but with no special authority or casting vote. Vanbrugh was reinstated as Comptroller and knighted, and Wren's elder son Christopher remained as Clerk Engrosser. Wren must have realized that his active life was nearly over—he never appeared before the commission after July 1715.

Meanwhile, the commissioners themselves ordered further "fittings" without reference to the Surveyor. The font was of veined Carrara marble carved by Francis Bird, with a wide shallow basin more suited to a Gargantua than any normal infant. The eagle lectern was of brass with lion's feet. There was a second litany desk, necessary repairs and adjustments were made to the clock, and Francis Bird was also commissioned to begin the carving of the seventeen statues needed for the west front and the north and south porticos. They were not completed until 1723. And the commissioners now revived a suggestion of the ironfounder Jones that the outer wall of the cathedral would be improved by a cast-iron balustrade. It was a suggestion which harked back to Inigo Jones' Banqueting House, and there were divided opinions as to whether iron or stone should be used. So far as Wren was concerned neither had been planned, and he wanted neither.

In October 1717, the commissioners arbitrarily decided upon a stone balustrade "except Sir Chr. Wren doe under his hand in writing declare it is contrary to the principles of Architecture". This was a direct challenge to Wren in his professional capacity on an issue of which he should have been sole judge. At 85 years of age he gave his forthright answer. In a memorandum to the commission dated 1 November 1717, he "took leave, first to declare that I never designed a balustrade" and proceeded to scorn "persons of little skill in architecture" who "did expect, I believe, to see something they had been used to in Gothic architecture, and ladies think nothing well without an edging". His irony was wasted on the commissioners, who impertinently referred the dispute to, of all people, Sir Isaac

Newton. Newton went to see Wren, and may have talked him
round; but in any event the balustrading, in stone, was soon in
hand, and today it would be a bold critic who maintained that
either side was wholly in the right.[4] What was crystal clear was
that Wren and his new masters by now were hopelessly at
loggerheads.

On 26 April 1718, the final blow fell. King George I deprived
Wren of his life appointment as Surveyor-General, and in his
place appointed a Whig politician named William Benson,
whose practice in architecture was confined to his own undistinguished house at Wilbury in Wiltshire. Wren retired, without
immediate protest, to live in the small house on Hampton
Green, near the gates of Hampton Court Palace, which had
been leased to him by Queen Anne. But a year later he was
constrained to write a remarkable letter to the Lords of the
Treasury which can speak for itself:

May it please yr Ldships,
My surprize is equal to my concern to find, that having
serv'd the Crown and the Publick above fifty years, and at
this great Age, I should be under a necessity of taking a part
in answering a memorial Presented by Mr Benson to your
Ldships chargeing some Mismanagement on the late Commissioners of the Board of Works.

It was his Majestie's Pleasure, on his happy accession to
the Throne to continue me in the Office of Surveyor of the
Works; but soon after, in regard of my great age, He was
Pleas'd of his Royal clemency to Ease me of the burden of
the Business of that office, by appointing other Worthy
Gentlemen with me in commission, which was under such
Regulations and Restrictions, as that altho' I had the honour
to be first nam'd with the old title of Surveyor, yet in acting
I had no power to over-rule, or give a casting Vote: I did
however as often as my Infirmities would permit, attend the
Board, and endeavour'd to doe his Majesty all the Service I
was able, with the same integrity and zeal which I had ever
practised.

I doubt not but the Gentlemen concern'd in the late
Commission will lay before yr Ldships such particular
answers to the Memorial of Complaint, as will be satisfactory;

I crave leave to Refer thereto; and may presume to say,
that notwithstanding the Pretensions of the Present Surveyor's Management to be better than that of the late
Commissioners, or theirs to be better than what Preceeded,
yet I am persuaded upon an impartial view of matters &
fairly distinguishing all particulars, with due consideration
had to long-protracted payment of artificers, there will be no
just grounds for the Censuring former Managements; and
as I am Dismiss'd, having worn out (by God's mercy) a long
Life in the Royal Service, and having made some Figure in
the World, I hope it will be allowed me to Die in Peace.

> I am, May it Please yr Ldships
> With most sincere Respect Yr Ldships most
> Obedient Humble Servant
> Chr. Wren.[5]

Only the signature was in Wren's own hand, and naturally it
was a trifle shaky.

In the following summer, it may have given Wren some
satisfaction that Benson was dismissed from his surveyorship
with ignominy for his incompetence; but by then Wren must
have been past caring. He was apparently well content to live
quietly by the river at Hampton, where he was able to take
up again some of the studies—especially those concerning
Saturn—which had absorbed him in his earlier days with the
Royal Society.[6] He was even able to complete a memorandum
on the subject of longitude which he wrote out in cypher.
Occasionally, he would journey to London by coach to his
house in St James's Street, and there, on 25 February 1723
after dinner, he was found by his manservant in the peaceful
sleep of death—he was in his ninety-first year.

In his will, Wren asked for a burial "without pomp", but it
was not to be. Even though in his final years his reputation
had been clouded by disputes, wrangles and libels, there was
no denying that the architect of St Paul's deserved a stately
funeral. The hearse from St James's Street was preceded by
"a handsome cavalcade", and followed by fifteen "mourning
coaches-and-six as well as several Gentlemen's coaches".[7] Only

in his tomb was Wren's last request fulfilled—he was buried
beneath a simple stone slab in the crypt of his cathedral along-
side his daughter. The inscription read in Latin: "Here lieth
Sir Christopher Wren Builder of This Cathedral Church of St.
Paul's etc who Died in the year of Our Lord MDCCXXIII and
of his age XCI", and above it his elder son ordered the engraving of a small marble tablet carrying in Latin the wording
"Below is laid the builder of this Church and City, Christopher
Wren, who lived above ninety years not for himself but for the
public good. Reader, if you seek a monument, look about you.
He died 25th Feb. 1723, in the 91st year of his life." The young
Christopher was no genius, but he deserves his mead of fame
as the author of the inspired and famous phrase: "Lector, si
monumentum requiris, Circumspice".[8]

Of Wren's personal appearance we can be reasonably certain.
In the Ashmolean Museum at Oxford is the superb marble bust
carved by Edward Pierce about 1673 when Wren was 41. It
was presented to the university by Wren's elder son in 1737.
The Royal Society, appropriately enough, possesses a good
portrait in oils painted by the German Johann Baptist Closter-
man about the year 1695 when Wren was 63. It was presented
to the society by Wren's grandson Stephen. In the Sheldonian
Theatre at Oxford is a portrait begun by Verrio and completed
by Thornhill and Kneller after Verrio's death in 1707—it
must therefore portray Wren at about 75. In the National
Portrait Gallery is the best-known portrait of all—the work
of Sir Godfrey Kneller painted in 1711 when Wren was nearing
80. Finally, there is the death mask at All Souls, Oxford; and
of less authentic portraits there is the Rysbrack bust at The
Queen's College, Oxford, dated 1727, which may have been
based on the death mask, and the boxwood plaque attributed
to Grinling Gibbons and now at the Royal Institute of British
Architects. All of these portraits agree in showing the handsome
features of a good-humoured intellectual, a touch of shyness and
a certain elegance;[9] and anyone who wishes to realize what
manner of man Wren was has only to stand for a few minutes
in front of the magical realism of Pierce's masterpiece in the
Ashmolean. For a literary description of Wren's appearance

there is the prose of John Ward, who in 1740 published a life of Wren in his book *Lives of the Professors of Gresham College*, and who was himself a Gresham professor of rhetoric. "He was low of stature," he writes, "thin, but by temperance and skilful management (for he was a proficient in anatomy and physic) he enjoyed a good state of health, and his life was protracted to an unusual length." On the other hand, it is known that Wren in his youth was delicate—which may have occasioned a special care for his general health which can partly account for his long and comparatively illness-free later life.[10]

Little is known of Wren's domestic life save the few bare facts which are already woven into the foregoing narrative. But something must be said about Christopher Wren, junior. He was, no doubt through his father's influence, appointed Chief Clerk of the Royal Works and Senior Clerk Engrosser from 1702 to 1716. He was first married to the daughter of Queen Anne's jeweller, and he seems to have been more interested in antique coins than in architecture, although there is a tradition that he was responsible for Marlborough House. He was a Member of Parliament for Windsor in 1714, but there is no other record of any political activities. He was responsible for collecting the Wren family papers, subsequently published by his son Stephen under the title of *Parentalia* in 1750. In 1715, he married as his second wife the widow of Sir Roger Burgoyne, Bart., of Wroxhall Abbey, Warwickshire, and his father was able to buy for him the fine Elizabethan house and estate at Wroxall for the considerable sum of £19,600.

Two letters of Sir Christopher to his elder surviving son exist.[11] The first reveals that the young Christopher had been sent on a visit to France in the company of master-mason Edward Strong's son "when you might make your observations and find acquaintance who might hereafter be usefull to you in the future concerns of life". The second finds him book-buying in Holland. Father and son seem always to have been on the best of terms, and young Christopher dutifully took care of his half-brother William.

The only intimate details of Wren's private life which have come down to us are mostly found in the diaries of his friend Robert Hooke. It was Samuel Pepys who best summed up the curious Mr Hooke—"who is the most and promises the least of any man in the world that I ever saw",[12] and Wren undoubtedly shared Pepys' view. They frequently dined together—the Rose, the Bear, the Ship and the Crown were some of their favourite hostelries—and jointly they "discovered" the delights of the theatre, including a performance of *The Tempest*. They took tobacco together at the coffee house, and enjoyed their claret and an occasional game of chess; and in spite of pressure of work they seem to have found the time to keep up their discussions on scientific subjects first mooted at the Royal Society.

Hooke records that in 1673 Wren was "sick with physic taking" and in 1675 "sick of the stone", and that there were some rare occasions when he was "surly", "not kind" and "even jealous of me"; but on the whole their friendship was warm and long-lasting. Hooke sent the young Christopher a hobby-horse for his birthday which cost him fourteen shillings and he gives the curious information that Wren cured worms "with burnt oyle", and actually "cured his Lady of the thrush by hanging a bag of live bog-lice about her neck". These are strange sidelights on the mathematician and rationalist philosopher, yet it is good to know that the great architect, like any ordinary man of his day, enjoyed his "beans and bacon", and was not averse to trying out stilt-walking at St Bartholomew's Fair.

Of Wren's private character and temperament there is the direct evidence of his friends. The *Tatler* of 1709 refers to his great "personal modesty";[13] Flamsteed finds him "the only honest person I have to deal with"; Dr Isaac Barrow, of Gresham College and later a pupil of Newton, writes of him "as one of whom it was doubtful whether he was most to be commended for the divine felicity of his genius or for the sweet humanity of his disposition—formerly as a boy prodigy, now as a man miracle, nay, even something superhuman", and it was Bishop Sprat who wrote that Wren "is so far from usurping the fame of other men that he endeavours with all care to conceal his own". Roger North, who was one of Wren's few critics, tells of how he and his brother Dudley used often to go to St Paul's "on Saturdays, which were Sir Chr. Wren's days, who was the Surveyor, and we commonly got a snatch of discourse with him who like a true philosopher was always obliging and communicative, and in every matter we enquired about gave short but satisfactory answers".[14] The encomiums of Evelyn have already been quoted, and only once—it occurs in a Treasury minute-book—was Wren ever accused of bad manners. He was charged with "insolence" for having forgotten to attend a committee meeting.

Of Wren's probity in a very lax age, despite the aspersions of the pamphleteers in later years, there is no doubt; and the unsolicited witness of his colleagues, who stoutly defended him against the Duchess of Marlborough's suspicions, was well deserved.[15] When Queen Anne was attempting to correct the licentiousness of the previous reigns, Wren supported her by issuing notices to his workmen that swearing on the cathedral site was sacrilege, and that in future culprits would be liable to instant dismissal—but whether there were any noticeable results will never be known.[16] And it was an admirable part of Wren's character that he was as meticulous over small affairs as he was conscientious over great. When reporting to William III on the state of Windsor Castle, he was careful to note that "where the jukes were emptied made the atmosphere very noisome to their Majesties' court",[17] and he was never too busy to take his part in the duty of searching for any new Guy Fawkes before the opening of Parliaments.[18]

Of Wren's leisure activities—and they cannot have had much scope in so busy a career—we learn that "he was unacquainted with tennis play",[19] but that he was fond of horse-riding when business affairs permitted. And although he had the greatest respect for his brother-in-law Dr Holder, who was a musician of note, and adored his daughter Jane who played the organ, there is no doubt that he himself was not greatly interested, as Pepys was, in either listening to or playing music. On the other hand, both as a scientist and as an architect, Wren obviously enjoyed using his pencil and his paint brushes—he was no mean performer with both. His dabbling in etching and aquatint and his excursion into landscape painting have already been noted.

In an age of dangerous political turmoil, Wren seems to have been exceptionally skilful and wise in keeping out of trouble. He was born a high Tory royalist, but he was never a politician and always a scientist—and on the only two occasions when he became a Member of Parliament his purpose was simply to help forward his projects at St Paul's. There is little doubt that over a period which covered a Commonwealth and five reigns Wren was as politically sceptical, and perhaps as cynical, as the celebrated Vicar of Bray; his own life-work was all the better for it.

From time to time there has been some controversy as to whether he was a Freemason, but there seems to be no firm evidence to prove that he ever joined that secret society, although there *is* evidence to show that his elder son may have done.[20]

As an educationist he was no revolutionary. Assuming that he himself was indeed at Westminster School, he nevertheless sent his son Christopher to Eton; yet he took a great interest in the curriculum and welfare of the Christ's Hospital schools.

It is difficult to estimate Sir Christopher Wren's means with accuracy. His salary at St Paul's was £200 a year, and his contract lasted for 36 years. For the Royal Hospital Chelsea he received an honorarium of £1,000. His monthly salary as Surveyor-General was £26.8.4 plus "riding charges" and a yearly livery fee, and he was in office from 1689 to 1718—nearly 30 years. It has been estimated that he received some £13,000 for his work on City churches, and in addition he received handsome presents in plate and cash from grateful City clients, and for his work at Oxford from Archbishop Sheldon.[21] Throughout his surveyorship, he had a free commodious house and offices in Scotland Yard. There is, therefore, no doubt that, although no Croesus, he was always comparatively well-off—he could not have helped to finance the Barbican scheme or bought the Wroxall estate for his elder son if his purse had not been tolerably well lined. The point that must be stressed is that he never inherited wealth—his income, whatever it may have totalled, was entirely earned by his own efforts.

In his own day, Wren achieved a double claim to fame—first as a scientist and second as an architect, and it was only in the late evening of his life that he tasted the bitterness of opposition and felt the pricks of criticism. Since his day, Wren's reputation has see-sawed. Already in his old age his architecture was looked at askance by the devotees of what is known as Palladianism—an architectural school led by Lord Burlington and his friends which grouped Wren with Hawksmoor and Vanbrugh as exponents of the over-theatrical and somewhat vulgar Baroque. Their own work, as exemplified in Burlington's Chiswick House, was coldly puritanical in its rigid adherence to the precepts and practice of Vitruvius, Palladio and Inigo Jones. On the other hand, James Gibbs, whose architectural writings in the first half of the eighteenth century became the Holy Writ of Palladianism, clearly owed much in his actual architecture to the inspiration of Wren's City churches, admired Wren personally and in the words of Sir John Summerson, "spread the Wren-type of church all over the English-speaking world".

In the mid-eighteenth century there was a curious revival of "Gothick" as seen in the whimsical conceit of Horace Walpole's Strawberry Hill, and Wren seemed forgotten. Towards the end of the century, the brothers Robert and James Adam brought new inspiration deriving from the Palace of Diocletian at Spalatto (now Split) and created Syon and Osterley, while Sir William Chambers revived Inigo Jones at Somerset House. Neither the Adam brothers nor Chambers owed anything to Wren, and John Nash at Regent Street and Regents Park was equally a stranger.

Yet, even in the eighteenth century, there were some signs of admiration—James Gandon's Custom House at Dublin (1781) was clearly inspired by Wren's Greenwich, Soufflot's Panthéon (1757) in Paris owed much to Wren's St Paul's, and the splendid parish church of Banbury in Oxfordshire (1790) by S. P. Cockerell is obviously descended from Wren's St Stephen's, Walbrook.

In the early years of the nineteenth century, Wren was once again on a pedestal, thanks largely to the enthusiasms of his first biographer James Elmes (1823) and of C. R. Cockerell, RA, who in 1838 composed the well-known picture which groups 60 of Wren's (attributed) creations in a single imaginary landscape—it was engraved by William Richardson and has frequently been reproduced since. But once again Wren's graph of fame dropped to zero—thanks to the propaganda of the Gothic Revivalists under Pugin and Ruskin. It was Pugin who described the classical style as "thrice cooked hashes of pagan fragments", and Ruskin who, in writing of "the foul torrent of the Renaissance", deplored a style "utterly devoid of all life, virtue, honourableness or power of doing good".

It remained for the Edwardians to restore Wren to his rightful position, and in doing so they may indeed have overstated their case. Much of the florid public architecture of the early twentieth century in England was supposed to be inspired by Wren—it was in fact a caricature. It was left to Sir Edwin Lutyens to strike a more sensible balance, and with the Wren bi-centenary celebrations of 1923 and the publications of the Wren Society which began in the following year, Wren's final position as one of the greatest of architects can be regarded as safe and assured.

That Wren was not only a great architect but also a distinguished pioneer of modern science and a wholly admirable personality it has been the pleasant purpose of this book to attempt to establish. Of the many tributes paid to him by his contemporaries perhaps the final words of John Ward are the most apt:

> He was modest, devout, strictly virtuous and very communicative of what he knew. And besides his peculiar eminency as an architect, so extensive was his learning and knowledge in all the polite arts, but especially the mathematics; his invention so fertil, and his discoveries so numerous and usefull; that he will always be esteemed a benefactor to mankind and an ornament to the age in which he lived.

Perhaps the most flattering of contemporary appreciations came from the pen of his friend John Evelyn, who, in dedicating his *Architects and Architecture* (London 1706) to Wren, proclaimed the:

> Esteem I have ever had of his Virtues and Accomplishments; not only in the Art of *Building* but through all the learned *Cycle* of the most useful *Knowledge* and abstruse sciences . . . if the whole *Art of Building* were lost, it might be recovered

and found again in *St Paul's*, the *historical Pillar* and those other *Monuments* of his happy *Talent* and Extraordinary *Genius*.

And, in modern times, it was the considered opinion of the distinguished historian H. A. L. Fisher that Wren was "probably the greatest Englishman since Shakespeare".[22] Wren's son tells us that the chosen motto of his father was "Numero Pondere et Mensura" which is a quotation from the Apocrypha's *Wisdom of Solomon*, and reads in English "but thou hast ordered all things in measure and number and weight".[23] The young Christopher comments that it was "a motto well adapted to a Mathematician"—he might with equal justice have added "or to an architect".

And when social historians castigate the follies and immoralities of the late seventeenth century they should also remember to pay tribute to the sober, modest yet prodigious achievements of a circle of contemporary English scholars whose greatest ornament was Sir Christopher Wren—geometer, astronomer and architect.

APPENDICES

APPENDIX A

A NEW CITY, new palaces, new university and college buildings, a new cathedral—these were Wren's major concerns; but he was never too busy to attend to the minor concerns of friends, and it is only proper to add a short appendix on Wren's less spectacular activities.

Many country houses and town mansions dating roughly from the Queen Anne or early Georgian period have at one time or another been attributed to Wren. In fact, only one country house and two town houses are known with certainty to have come from his drawing board.

At Tring, in Hertfordshire, there is evidence that, in or about 1670, he built a country house for one Henry Guy, who was a favourite Gentleman of the Privy Chamber to Charles II and later Secretary to the Treasury. A signed plan of this house has survived although the house itself has gone, and an engraved elevation of it was made by John Oliver, one of Wren's deputies at St Paul's.[1] It is also true that at All Souls there is an authentic Wren drawing which shows both the plan and the elevation of a large country mansion with four corner pavilions and short colonnades linking a central block to lesser stable and service blocks on either hand. It is not known that it was ever constructed, but its design can be seen as the prototype for many English country houses of the following century.[2]

Wren's earlier town house was the deanery at St Paul's which has been described in chapter VI.[3] Towards the end of his life, Wren built a larger town house—this time for the redoubtable Sarah, Duchess of Marlborough—next door to St James's Palace.[4] It was built between 1709 and 1711 in red brick (specially imported from Holland) with stone dressings. Its original proportions have been ruined by attic storeys and a projecting entrance block added in the nineteenth century.

The present Marlborough House does not deserve to be associated with the original architect's name, and there may be
truth in the story that Wren's son Christopher had more to do
with it than his father.

As Surveyor-General, Wren was constantly in touch concerning financial matters with the Secretary to the Treasury—
one William Lowndes. Wren was said to have been involved
in the original design for this gentleman's country mansion—
Winslow Hall, Buckinghamshire, but the extent of his involve-
ment is not known.[5] At Arbury Hall, Warwickshire, it is known
that Wren designed a doorway carrying the escutcheon of the
Newdigate family, but it no longer survives.[6] At Easton Neston,
Northamptonshire, Wren certainly contributed to the original
house built for Sir William Fermor, privy councillor to Charles
II but his share in the work has been completely lost in the
subsequent rebuilding by Hawksmoor.[7] Wren took a great
interest in both the accommodation and the curriculum of
Christ's Hospital, London. In 1692 he supervised drawings for
a new writing school named after Sir John Moore, but the
detailed work was done by Hawksmoor.[8] At Appleby in
Leicestershire Wren designed Sir John Moore's Writing School
in 1693–7 but the work was carried out—and completely
altered—by Sir William Wilson.[9] At Windsor, Wren supervised
the completion of the elegant Court House after the death of
its designer and part-builder Sir Thomas Fitz in 1689.[10] At
Westminster in 1706 Wren rearranged the House of Commons
in order to provide for the additional 45 Scottish Members
created by the Act of Union.[11]

Of churches associated with Wren by tradition there is a
longer list, but again there is little to be said. At Ingestre in
Staffordshire, a friend and fellow member of the Royal Society,
Mr Walter Chetwynd, owned a "Jacobethan" country house
of some distinction, and a drawing in the Wren collections
shows a lantern design for the nearby church of St Mary's
labelled "Mr Chetwynd's Tower". It is a slim excuse for
attaching Wren's name to this simple church, and in fact the
tower was never built.[12] At the parish church of St Mary's in
Warwick, after a disastrous fire in 1694, Wren was asked to
plan rebuilding, and several unfinished drawings exist to illustrate his ideas for the tower, together with a dramatic perspec-

tive impression of the whole exterior which was probably drawn by Dickinson. The present tower owes very little to Wren—it was the work of Sir William Wilson, a local "statuary", and is a curious mixture of Renaissance influence working on a Gothic base.[13] Fortunately, the fire of 1694 did no damage to the superb effigies of the Beauchamp Chapel. At Ely Cathedral—where Wren's long-suffering uncle had been bishop until 1667—Wren gave technical advice in connection with repairs to the north transept, and a doorway there of no great merit is still attributed to him, although it was probably the design of the contracting mason Robert Grumbold.[14] At Ampthill church, Bedfordshire, Wren was involved in a design for the family pew of Lord Ashburnham, but it no longer exists.[15] At St Martin-in-the-Fields, Westminster—Wren's own parish church—Wren designed a "cupola" for the tower in 1672, but in 1722 it was demolished and the church was completely rebuilt by James Gibbs.[16] At St George's Chapel, Windsor, Wren reported on the state of the fabric in 1681–2, and supervised the consequent repairs.[17] In the Public Record Office there is a plan and elevation for enlarging the French Protestant Church in the Savoy dated 1686.[18] At St Margaret's, Westminster, he was called on to advise on a gallery for the south aisle in 1682, but this was subsequently demolished by Sir Gilbert Scott in 1877.[19] At the ancient Temple church, Wren repaired the fabric and refitted the interior in 1682–3. In 1840 his reredos and other fittings were removed to the Bowes Museum at Castle Barnard in County Durham, but recently they have been rightly restored to their original site.[20]

It is perhaps remarkable that Wren never built a house for himself—or his family—but he *was* involved in a domestic building project with many of his colleagues at St Paul's. A fire in 1687 had destroyed Bridgewater House in the Barbican of London, and in the following year the site was bought by Wren and George Jackson of Chipping Warden for £4,400. It was their intention to develop the site for domestic buildings and plots were actually taken up by Hawksmoor, Wren's assistant, William Emmett bricklayer, Samuel Fulkes mason, Henry Doogood plasterer, Nicholas Goodwin brickmaker, Richard Billinghurst bricklayer, and Samuel Wing ironmonger. Apparently, the Earl of Bridgewater had commissioned Wren in 1673 to lay-out the site for just such a development, but it had not been carried out. In June 1673, a royal warrant approved a second scheme, and work went ahead. Unfortunately, neither details nor drawings remain of Wren's only known venture into property development.[21] There is an intriguing tradition that the William and Mary College at Williamsburg in Virginia, USA, was built to an exported design of Wren's, and it is certain that English craftsmen and materials were used. The tradition cannot be substantiated, and the original building was destroyed by fire in 1705 and redesigned by local architects.[22]

There, then, is the somewhat meagre list of Wren's work in less spectacular fields. It is sad that modern research has had to delete from his *oeuvre* such famous and such admirable buildings as Morden College, Blackheath, the Seth Ward almshouses and Mompesson House at Salisbury, the John Edes and the Dodo houses at Chichester, old Temple Bar in London and All Saints church, Northampton. It is, however, one measure of Wren's greatness that some of the best in so many fields has frequently been wrongly attributed to his invention

APPENDIX B

In October 1748, "the curious and entire libraries of that ingenious architect Sir Christopher Wren Kt. and Christopher Wren, Esq." were sold in London.

An analysis of the catalogue shows the following classifications:

Books of Engravings (mostly of Rome)	– 126	volumes
Antiquities (Classical 37, British 11)	– 48	volumes
Travel and Topography	– 45	volumes
Tracts (of various kinds)	– 43	volumes
"Modern" History (including Froissart)	– 28	volumes
Architecture	– 21	volumes
Mathematics	– 21	volumes
Philosophy and Science	– 20	volumes
Religion	– 19	volumes
Astronomy	– 17	volumes
Classics (Latin and Greek)	– 11	volumes
Natural History	– 7	volumes
Music	– 5	volumes
Fortifications	– 3	volumes
Reference	– 3	volumes

REFERENCES

REFERENCES

The following abbreviations are used throughout:
CUP=Cambridge University Press.
OUP=Oxford University Press.
Par.=*Parentalia*, or *Memoirs of the Family of the Wrens* by Christopher Wren (II) and published by his son Stephen Wren in 1750. The references are to the fascimile edition of the so-called "heirloom" copy in the possession of the RIBA and reprinted in 1965 by the Gregg Press of Farnborough.
BV=*Sir Christopher Wren 1632–1723* (Bicentenary Memorial Volume) published by Hodder & Stoughton on behalf of the RIBA in London in 1923, ed. Rudolf Dircks.
WS=The twenty volumes published by the *Wren Society* at Oxford from 1924–1943, eds. A. T. Bolton and H. D. Hendry.

Chapter 1

1 There were 11 children in all. Some confusion has arisen because of a son Christopher born dead in 1631. Dean Wren recorded the dates of all his family on the fly-leaf of his copy of Helwig's *Theatrum Historicum* (1618) now in the National Museum of Wales.
2 The Act of Uniformity of 1661 enforced the reading of Morning and Evening Prayer, and the Sunday Observance Act of 1667 prohibited all trade, business and travel on Sundays.
3 *Par.*, 142.
4 cp. E. F. Sekler, *Wren and His Place in European Architecture*, Faber, London, 1956, 26–7.
5 An estimate for £13,305 dated 16 May 1635, is reproduced by J. Elmes in his *Memoirs of the Life and Works of Sir Christopher Wren*, Priestley and Weale, London, 1823. cp. L. Phillimore, *Sir Christopher Wren*, Kegan Paul, London, 1881, 40; *BV*, 14.
6 *Par.*, 183.
7 *Par.*, 181.
8 The usual date quoted is 1649, but this is a mistake: cp. *Wadham College* MS 110/2.

9   *Par.*, 135–6.
10 J. Aubrey, *Brief Lives*, ed. A. Powell, Cape, London, 1949, 180.
11 *Par.*, 181.
12 *Par.*, 185. Nothing is known of the nature of the illness.
13 *Par.*, 182–7, 198–9, 215, and Illustrations 5 and 6 and between pp. 226–7.
14 There are two surviving sundials at Bletchingdon—one on the church porch, and one in the stable yard of Bletchingdon Park, both of which are attributed with some probability to the young Wren.
15 The models were destroyed in the Great Fire of London, 1666. *Par.*, 187.
16 *Par.*, 187–93.

Chapter II

1   P. A. Wright-Henderson, *The Life and Times of John Wilkins*, OUP, Oxford, 1910, passim; J. Aubrey, op. cit., 320; J. Evelyn, *Diary*, 13 July 1654; S. Pepys, *Diary*, 12 February 1664. Wren is reputed to have constructed Wadham's college clock—the face is still at the college, the works are in the Museum of the History of Science.
2   *Par.*, 182–3. Wren took over Ward's oriel room over the main gateway to Wadham in October 1663.
3   I am indebted to C. S. L. Davies Esq., Keeper of the Archives at Wadham College, for these facts and figures.
4   *Par.*, 215–16.
5   J. Evelyn, *Diary*, 24 October 1664—"that incomparable genius and my worthy friend".
6   *Par.*, 214. "A neat piece of work", says Sir Robert Plot in his *Natural History of Oxfordshire*, Oxford, 1677, 269.
7   *Par.*, 210.
8   *Par.*, between pp. 226 and 227
9   *Par.*, 227–38.
10 *Par.*, 217–19.
11 In T. Willis, *Cerebri Anatome Nervorum Descriptio et Usus*, Geneva, 1680.
12 Robert Hooke, *Micrographia or Physiological Descriptions of Minute Bodies made by the help of Magnifying Glasses*, London, 1665. cp. *Par.*, 212.
13 *Par.*, 213–14. *Parentalia* maintains that Wren was the first inventor of the mezzotint. In fact, it was first invented by Ludwig von Siegen of Utrecht in 1624. There are two mezzotint heads of a

negro boy in the British Museum print-room attributed to Wren.
cp. A. M. Hind, *A Short History of Engraving*, Constable, London,
1908, 258, n.1.

14 J. Harrington, *The Prerogative of Popular Government*, London,
1658, and M. Wren, *Monarchy Asserted*, London, 1659.

15 *Par.*, 255–6; J. Elmes, *Sir Christopher Wren and His Times*,
London, 1852, 56.

16 J. Morgan, *Phoenix Britannicus*, London, 1732, 247. For Wren's
verses see *News from the Dead*, 2nd ed. Oxford, 1651, 13–14.

17 cp. Aytoun Ellis, *The Penny Universities*, Secker & Warburg,
London, 1956, passim: "So great a Universitie/I think there ne'er
was any/In which you may a scholar be/For spending of a penny"
(contemporary rhyme).

18 Thomas Sprat, *The History of the Royal Society of London for the
Improving of Natural Knowledge*, London, 1667, 53–4.

19 H. A. L. Fisher, *Pages from the Past*, OUP, Oxford, 1939, VII—
"The real Oxford Movement".

20 *Par.*, 33–4.

21 B. Pascal, *Oeuvres*, Paris, 1819, V 129 ff. Wren's paper on the
cycloid was published by Dr Wallis in his *Opera Mathematica*, Oxford,
1695, I 533–41. cp. R. T. Gunther, *Early Science in Oxford*, OUP,
Oxford, 1923, I 117 ff. and V. Fürst, *The Architecture of Sir Christopher
Wren*, Lund Humphries, London, 1956, p. 217, n. 934; A. R. Hinks
in *BV*, 239–54.

22 *Par.*, 198–9.

Chapter III

1 cp. John Ward, *Lives of the Professors of Gresham College*, London
1740, 95–111.

2 The Latin version is in Ward op. cit. and in *Par.*, 220–7. A
translation is in Wetton, Jarvis and Whiteley, *Select Biography*,
London, 1822, IV. The English version is in *Par.*, 200–6, and cp. *BV*,
248 for Wren's "nebulae" theories.

3 *Par.*, 254–5.

4 *The Life of Anthony à Wood*, Oxford, 1730, 559; *Par.*, 213.

5 The first history of the Royal Society is T. Sprat's op. cit. He
ascribed its origin to the Oxford meetings of the 1650s. In 1678, John
Wallis, Savilian professor of geometry at Oxford, first launched the
story that the true origin of the RS was in the meetings of a group of
scientists in London in 1640. This theory received official approval
in T. Birch, *History of the Royal Society*, London, 1756, and has been

sanctioned until recently. Margery Purver's *The Royal Society, Concept and Creation*, Royal Society, London, 1967, restores the authority of Sprat. It is true that the "Invisible College" of Robert Boyle (cp. Robert Boyle, *Works*, ed. T. Birch, London, 1772, I 20) existed in London during the period 1646–8, and its membership certainly included some of the later Oxford group round Wilkins, but its aims were purely utilitarian. Aubrey in *Brief Lives*, ed. A. Clark, OUP, Oxford, 1898, II 300, agrees with Sprat. The whole controversy is based on the original error of Wallis, which he himself later corrected.

6   cp. Dorothy Stimson, *Scientists and Amateurs*, Sigma, London, 1949, pl. 7.

7   *Instructions concerning erecting a Library* by Gabriel Naudens (Naudé), trans. J. Evelyn, London, 1661.

8   *Par.*, 196–7.

9   cp. Sprat, op. cit., 62–7 and 113; *Cambridge Modern History*, V, 740–1.

10   B. de Monconys, *Voyages d'Angleterre*, ed. M. C. Henry, Paris, 1887, 61–76; "grand Mathématicien quoy que petit de corps".

11   *Par.*, 211–13.

12   *Par.*, 260.

13   cp. Sir Jonas Moore, *System of Mathematics*, London, 1681, 573. For Wren's work on the moon, see G. H. Turnbull, *Notes and Records of the Royal Society*, Royal Society, London, 1953, V 116, and A. R. Hinks in *BV*, 250–1.

14   cp. Robert Hooke, *Comets* in his posthumous *Works*, London, 1705, 104; J. Elmes, *Memoirs* op. cit., app., 60.

15   T. Sprat, op. cit., 57–8; R. T. Gunther, op. cit., I 317–22; *Par.*, 222–4.

16   cp. J. Wallis op. cit., I 533–41.

17   I. Newton, *Principia*, trans. A. Motte, London, 1729, I 32; T. Sprat, op. cit., 318.

18   For Wren's minor "inventions" see R. T. Gunther, op. cit., 215–17, 231, 274, 276 and S. Pepys, *Diary*, 30 April 1669.

Chapter IV

1   cp. J. H. Harvey, *Henry Yevele*, Batsford, London, 1944; D. Knoop and G. P. Jones, *The Mediaeval Mason*, Manchester University Press, 1933, passim; N. Pevsner on *The Term Architect in the Middle Ages* in *Speculum* XVII 1942, 549–62.

2   J. Summerson, *Architecture in Britain, 1530–1830*, Penguin, London, 1969, 28–9 and 555.

3 J. Dent, *The Quest for Nonsuch*, Hutchinson, London, 1962, passim.

4 J. Summerson, *Inigo Jones*, Penguin, London, 1966, passim.

5 cp. S. Pepys, *Diary*, 1 February 1663/4, where Charles II laughs at Gresham College "for spending time only in weighing of ayre and doing nothing else since they sat".

6 cp. G. F. Webb, *The Architectural Antecedents of Sir Christopher Wren* in *RIBA Jnl.*, XL May 1933.

7 R. J. Gunther, *The Architecture of Sir Roger Pratt*, OUP, 1928; cp. J. Evelyn, *Diary*, 10 June 1684.

8 *Par.*, 335–9 summarizes the construction and pays full tribute to Wallis. cp. *WS*, XIX 126 ff.

9 When Pepys saw Streeter's work, he noted (*Diary*, 1 February 1668/9) "the rest think better than those of Rubens in the Banqueting-house at White Hall, but I do not so fully think so".

10 cp. *RIBA Jnl.* XXX 264. On the other hand, Defoe in his *Tour through England and Wales*, described the Sheldonian as "infinitely superior to anything in the world of its kind".

11 For the somewhat academic controversy about the respective dates of the Sheldonian and Pembroke Chapel, see V. Fürst, op. cit., 182, 23.

12 For Wren's Paris visit cp. M. Whinney in *Gazette des Beaux Arts*, 1958, 229–42; *WS*, V 140 and XIII 17, 40–1; *Par.*, 261–8.

13 R. Boyle, op. cit., VI 191, where Wren is reported to have been "well received" at Paris, and to have been present at some of the meetings of the Académie.

14 See letter 30 September 1665 in *WS*, XVIII 180 and E. P. Warren in *BV*, 233–8.

15 *Par.*, 350–66.

16 *Par.*, 273–7.

17 *WS*, I pls. iv–viii and XIII 17.

18 In the National Portrait Gallery is a portrait of Charles II by Henry Danckerts showing the royal gardener presenting the King with a pineapple; cp. S. Sitwell, *British Architects and Craftsmen*, Batsford, London, 1948, 58–9; *WS*, XIX 149, pl. xxii; plate facing p. 232 of *BV* showing sketch for a much "pineappled" Pembroke Chapel; E. F. Sekler, op. cit., 111; *WS*, I v–viii. St Paul's has gilded pineapples on top of each of the western towers.

19 *WS*, XII 44–5.

20 J. Evelyn, *Diary*, 27 August 1666. Evelyn has frequently been mis-read—he does *not* say that the cupola design was accepted; cp. V. Fürst, op. cit., 187, n. 164.

Chapter V

1 For the Great Fire, cp. J. Evelyn, *Diary*, 2–7 September 1666; S. Pepys, *Diary*, 2–14 September 1666; W. G. Bell, *The Great Fire of London in 1666*, John Lane, London, 1920, passim.

2 S. Pepys, *Diary*, 26 September 1666.

3 S. Pepys, *Diary*, 3 and 13 February 1667.

4 T. F. Reddaway, *The Rebuilding of London after the Great Fire*, Cape, London, 1940, passim.

5 For Wren's plan, see *Par.*, 267; S. Perks in *RIBA Jnl.* XXVII 69–82; E. F. Sekler, op. cit., 58.

6 *Par.*, 269; but Hawksmoor was also responsible for the legend, see V. Fürst, op. cit., 183, n. 54; *WS*, VI 17–27.

7 A. Bryant, *Letters, Speeches and Declarations of King Charles II*, Collins, London, 1935, 191–4.

8 R. Hooke, *Diary, 1672–1680*, ed. H. W. Robinson and F. Adams, Taylor & Francis, London, 1935; M. I. Batten, *The Architecture of Dr Robert Hooke* in *Walpole Soc.*, XXV (1937) 844; M. 'Espinasse, *Robert Hooke*, Heinemann, London, 1956.

9 *WS*, V 14–16, pls. iv–v.

10 R. J. Wallis and J. W. Clark, *The Architectural History of the University of Cambridge*, CUP, Cambridge, 1886, II 703–9; *WS*, V 29–31, pl. xii.

11 *Par.*, 303–6; *WS*, XI 21–6.

12 *WS*, XIII, 20–2.

13 *Par.*, 278–9.

14 S. Pepys, *Diary*, 21 March 1669.

15 *WS*, XVIII 187, pl. vi; *Cal. of Treasury Books* III (1) 74.

16 J. Evelyn, *Diary*, 9 July–14 August 1669; *WS*, IX 39 and X 129. For the Bodleian repairs see E. F. Warren in *BV*, 233–8.

17 *Par.*, pl. 9 and *WS*, XIX 152–3.

Chapter VI

1 cp. T. F. Reddaway, op. cit., passim.

2 *WS*, IX and X passim.

3 cp. G. Cobb, *London City Churches*, City of London, 1951; G. H. Birch, *London Churches of the 17th and 18th Centuries*, Batsford, London, 1896.

4 *Par.*, 318–21. Wren also had strong views on pews—"it were to be wished there were to be no pews but benches; but there is no stemming the tide of profit and the advantage of pew-keepers".

5 *Par.*, 278–80; *WS*, XIII 22–3 and 46–8; *St Paul's Minute Book*, 4 August 1668 (Guildhall).

6 *Par.*, 283–92. For the whole story, Joan Lang's brilliant *The Rebuilding of St Paul's after the Great Fire of London*, OUP, Oxford, 1956, is indispensable.

7 cp. Norbert Lynton, *A Wren Drawing for St Paul's* in *Burlington Mag.*, February 1955, XCVII 40–4.

8 cp. Fürst, op. cit., 30–3 and notes; R. T. Gunther, op. cit., 213. The St Paul's building accounts are full of references to the cost of "modells"—there was even a model made for an engine to lift seven-ton blocks over 100 feet.

9 *Par.*, 282; J. M. W. Halley on *Rebuilding St Paul's* in *RIBA Jnl.*, XXII (1915) 49–60, 73–82.

10 V. Fürst, op. cit., 35–6; *Apollo*, October 1968.

11 *WS*, XVIII 193, note. But Christopher Wren jun. in a letter to John Ward dated 24 January 1740 wrote "I have no account of the exact time when he was knighted . . . there can be little or no mistake to assign the time to the year 1674", *Sloane Coll.*, BM, cp. V. Fürst, op. cit., 190–1, n. 225.

12 *Par.*, 282.

13 *Par.*, 285; V. Fürst, op. cit., 38–41.

14 *Par.*, 283.

15 *Par.*, 292.

16 cp. R. Leacroft on *Wren's Drury Lane* in *Arch. Rev.* July 1950; *WS*, XII, pl. xxiii.

17 cp. M. I. Batten, op. cit., 85–6.

18 *WS*, XVII 76–7, pl. lxv–lxvi.

Chapter VII

1 T. F. Reddaway, op. cit., 216, n.; *Par.*, 321–4; M. I. Batten, op. cit., 84; *WS*, V 45–51, pl. xxxiv–xxxvi; W. G. Bell, op. cit., 208–9, and in *RIBA Jnl* XLVII (1918) 117; for Cibber and the Monument see *MS 5761 Guildhall*.

2 *PRO* Works 5/145 p. 99; *WS*, V 52 and pl. xxxviii.

3 *WS*, XIX 113–15; pl. lxviii–lxix.

4 cp. W. D. Caröe, *Tom Tower, Oxford* OUP, Oxford, 1923, passim.

5 Willis and Clark op. cit., II 538–51; *WS*, V 32–44, pl. xv–xxvi; H. M. Fletcher on *Sir Christopher Wren's Carpentry*, in *RIBA Jnl* (3rd series) XXX (1923) 388.

6 *WS*, V 18, XIX 100–2.

7 *Par.*, 330–2; V. Fürst, op. cit., 107–9 and notes; *WS*, XIX 52–4.

8 *BV*, 85.

9 J. Evelyn, *Diary*, 20 April 1673; 3 September 1676; 1 August 1682; J. Lang op. cit., 93 ff.

10 T. F. Reddaway, op. cit., 186–7.

11 cp. W. Dugdale, *The History of St Paul's Cathedral in London* ed. H. Ellis, London, 1818, 42–68.

12 See Minutes of St Paul's Commission for 23 December 1680 and report dated March 1679 at Guildhall Library. cp. J. Lang, op. cit., 103–16.

13 For the Warrant Design cp. *WS*, I pl. lx–lxiii.

14 Could Wren not have obtained the extra width and weight of walling while still keeping the aisles to the original Warrant Design width?

15 cp. J. Summerson on *The Penultimate Design for St Paul's* in *Burlington Mag.*, March 1961, CIII 839.

16 cp. Somers Clark in *BV*, 73–82.

17 cp. Sir William Schooling on *Sir Christopher Wren, Merchant Adventurer* in *BV* 257–64.

18 cp. *Country Life*, 28 May 1948, 1073.

19 W. D. Caröe, op. cit., passim; WS, V 17–23, pl. viii, and XIX, pl. liv–lvi.

20 cp. C. G. T. Dean, *The Royal Hospital Chelsea*, Hutchinson, London, 1950; *Par.*, 327; *WS*, XIX 61–86, pl. xxx–xlvii.

21 *Par.*, 318–21.

22 J. Evelyn, *Diary*, 17 April 1684/5.

23 *Par.*, 157; *WS*, VII 11–69 and 233, pl. l–lv; V. Fürst, op. cit., 75–6; *BV* 154–5; A. T. Bolton in *RIBA Jnl* XXXVII November 1929, 43–8.

24 Celia Fiennes, *Journeys Through England*, ed. C. Morris, Cresset, London, 1947, wrote "I saw the Modell, very fine but it is never like to be finished now."

25 cp. *WS*, X 43.

Chapter VIII

1 *Par.*, 344; J. Lang, op. cit., 125; *WS*, XVI 78, 90, 98.

2 *WS*, VII 71–9, pl. vii, xiii–xvi, and VIII, pl. i–x.

3 J. Evelyn, *Diary*, 29 December 1686.

4 The steps are in the Whitehall Gardens to the west of Hungerford Bridge.

5 *WS*, XVIII 187, pl. v.

6 J. Lang, op. cit., 137; *WS*, XIV 80, 123, 136.

7 *Par.*, 326–7; *WS*, IV passim; E. Law, *History of Hampton Court Palace*, London, 1855, 91.

8 cp. M. Whinney on *William Talman* in *Jnl. of Warburg and Courtauld Insts.*, XVIII (1955) 1–2.

9 *WS*, VII 135–96 and plates.

10 *Par.*, 327.

11 *WS*, V 14–16, pl. iv–v.

12 M. E. Macartney in *BV*, 69–72; V. Fürst, op. cit., 201, n. 572.

13 It was useful to Wren that at this time his brother-in-law, Dr Holder, had become a member of the Cathedral Chapter.

14 Roger North, *Lives of the Norths*, Bohn, London, 1890, II 238; H. M. Colvin on *Roger North and Sir Christopher Wren* in *Arch. Rev.* CX, October 1951, 257–60.

15 *WS*, V 18 and IX 100–2; for C. Kempster cp. W. D. Caröe, op. cit., 82–8; for the Strongs and the Kempsters cp. D. Knoop and G. P. Jones, *The London Mason in the 17th century*, Manchester University Press, Manchester, 1935.

16 R. Lane Poole, *Edward Pierce the Sculptor* in *Walpole Soc.* XI (1923) 34; J. Seymour on *Edward Pearce, Baroque Sculptor of London*, in *Guildhall Misc.* I (1952) 10; J. Lang, op. cit., 113–14.

17 D. B. Green, *Grinling Gibbons; his work as Carver and Statuary*, Country Life, London, 1964; H. A. Tipping, *Grinling Gibbons and the Woodwork of his Age*, Country Life, London, 1950; J. Evelyn, *Diary*, 18 January 1671; for Gibbons at his worst see the Sir Cloudesley Shovel memorial in Westminster Abbey. For a more generous view cp. J. Lang, op. cit., 166 ff.

18 cp. R. Gunnis, *Dictionary of British Sculptors 1660–1851*, Odhams, London, 1953.

19 *BV*, 98, 106, fig. 12; W. G. Hiscock on *Jonathan Maine, Woodcarver* in *Country Life*, 31 December 1948. *WS*, XVI 81.

20 H. Faber, *Caius Gabriel Cibber*, OUP, Oxford, 1926; J. Lang, op. cit., 209.

21 R. Gunnis, op. cit., 54. The Queen Anne statue at the west front of St Paul's was erected to commemorate the final completion of the building in 1711. It was badly mutilated by a lunatic who said it libelled his mother. In 1886, a copy in Sicilian marble was begun by Richard Bolt, who died before he could finish it. The original, rescued from the yard of a City stonemason, was bought by Augustus Hare, and re-erected on his estate at Holmhurst St Mary, Baldslow, St Leonards-on-Sea, where it can still be seen inspiring the girl's school of the Community of the Holy Family.

22 cp. S. Sitwell, op. cit., 78. Tijou's forge was at Hampton Court; he was also responsible for the metalwork of the huge windows at the Cathedral.

23   H. S. Goodhart-Rendel, *Nicholas Hawksmoor*, London, 1924; K. Downes, *Hawksmoor*, London, 1959.

24   cp. J. Lang, op. cit., 139–40. A very rare case of insubordination is noted in the long-lost *Minute Book of the Royal Commission on St Paul's*, MS 11770, Guildhall: "Several of the Artificers and their workmen have been disorderly refusing to be obedient to Order and directions for staying within the work at Breakfast time . . . dismissed and turn'd out". 17 June 1680.

25   J. Lang, op. cit., 175–6; *WS*, XIV 147.

26   *Par.*, 320, 357.

27   J. Lang, op. cit., 240; E. J. Hopkins and E. F. Rimbault, *The Organ, its History and Construction*, London, 1835.

28   J. Lang, op. cit., 195. Wren's wooden "trolley" has disappeared. The present pulpit was designed by Lord Mottistone and first used in 1964—it does not flatter modern craftsmanship. It replaced the marble pulpit (by Penrose) of 1861 now re-erected in the crypt.

29   A. T. Bolton in *RIBA Jnl* XLIII (1936) 593; N. Pevsner, *The Buildings of England, London I*, Penguin, London, 1957, 126.

30   J. Lang, op. cit., 198–202, 224–5; *WS*, XVI 86–9.

31   J. Lang, op. cit., 248.

Chapter IX

1   *Par.*, 327–9; *WS*, VI, passim.

2   cp. *WS*, XVIII 166, where Wren obtains recognition for one of his workmen who helped him.

3   *WS*, XVI 95.

4   cp. H. Faber, *Caius Gabriel Cibber*, OUP, Oxford, 1926.

5   J. Lang, op. cit., 217–18.

6   *WS*, XV 49, XVI 93.

7   J. Lang, op. cit., 233.

8   J. Lang, op. cit., 232–3.

9   For Wren's knowledge of domes see V. Fürst, op. cit., 139–41 and 719, 734; Wren's *Tract II* in *Par.*, 353–4; *WS*, XIX 131–2. Wren had de Rossi's *Insignium* (1684) in his library—he therefore was probably aware of all the seventeenth-century domes. For his use of cones in steeples cp. *BV*, 33–4; J. Lang, op. cit., 215–16, 233.

10   J. Lang, op. cit., 234–5; cp. J. Ruskin, *Seven Lamps of Architecture* (Everyman) 224–8—"I think it better work to bind a tower with iron than to support a false dome by a brick pyramid".

11   J. Lang, op. cit., 151–2, 245.

12   *WS*, XV 148, XVI 10; S. A. Alexander in *BV*, 93 and 265–70; K. Downes, *Christopher Wren*, Penguin, London, 1971, 172; M. Whinney, *Wren*, Thames & Hudson, London, 1971, 122; S. B. Hamilton on *The Place of Sir Christopher Wren in the History of Structural Engineering* in *Trans. of the Newcomen Soc.* XIV (1933–4) 27–42.

13   J. Lang, op. cit., 240.

14   *WS*, XIII 57–8; J. Lang, op. cit., 273–9.

15   *WS*, XVI 108–11 and 155.

16   *Par.*, 292; *WS*, XIV 109; J. Lang, op. cit., 247 and 252.

17   J. Evelyn, *Diary*, 7 September 1704.

18   *Par.*, 293—The basket legend is based on the Duchess of Marlborough's complaint against Vanbrugh's expensiveness at Blenheim. She contrasted it with Wren's economy at Marlborough House. Wren, she said, was "a pattern of moderation—content to be dragged up in a basket three or four times a week to the top of St Paul's and at great hazard for £200 a year". cp. C. Fiennes, op. cit., 291, n. 13; M. S. Briggs, *Christopher Wren*, Allen & Unwin, London, 1951; J. Lang, op. cit., 236. That the basket still exists at St Paul's is a myth.

19   cp. D. Piper, *The Companion Guide to London*, Collins, London, 1964, 274—"a madrigal in stone".

20   J. Lang, op. cit., 248.

21   In December 1705/6, Jennings had received a gratuity "for his skill and extraordinary Pains Care and Diligence in the performance of the Centring of the Dome and for Modells of the same —fifty guineas".

Chapter X

1   *WS*, 141–53.

2   *Par.*, 295–302; V. Fürst, op. cit., 170; *WS*, XI 12–34, pl. i–vi.

3   *Par.*, 352 (26 April 1718).

4   *WS*, XVI 106–33; *Minute Bk of St Paul's*, at Guildhall library, 1 November 1717.

5   There is a tradition that George I's unpopular mistress Countess Schulenberg—promoted to Duchess of Kendal—persuaded him to dismiss Wren. cp. *Par.*, 344 and *Cal. of State Papers*, CCXX, 48, p. 448, 21 April 1719.

6   For Wren's Hampton Court home, which was leased to him by Queen Anne, see *WS*, XII 20, pl. xx; *Par.*, 344–6.

7   *Weekly Journal* No. 2491, Saturday 9 March 1723.

8   The famous phrase is now repeated in the pavement under the

dome. The full inscription above the tomb reads "Subtus Conditur Huius Ecclesiae et Urbis Conditor Christophorus Wren Qui Vixit Annos Ultra Nonaginta Non Sibi sed Bon Publico, Lector, Si Monumentum Requiris, Circumspice. Obiit XXV Feb, Ann MDCCXXIII Aet XCI." On the stone grave-slab is the inscription "Here lieth Sir Christopher Wren Kt. Builder of this Cathedral Church of St Paul's etc. who Died in the year of our Lord MDCCXXIII and of his age XCI". Miss Lang's translation of the Latin is: "Below is laid the builder of this Church and City, Christopher Wren, who lived above ninety years, not for himself but for the public good. Reader, if you seek a monument, look about you. He died 25 Feb. 1723 in the 91st year of his life."

9   In the library at St Paul's there is a small piece of one of Wren's "waistcoats" in blue and white flowered satin; and there is also his measuring rod six feet long.

10   J. Ward, op. cit.; *Par.*, 346 and 348; *BV*, 28.

11   *Par.*, between 194 and 195.

12   S. Pepys, *Diary*, op. cit., 9, 10, 12, 13, 16, 27, 60, 67, 87, 108, 116, 127, 156, 163, 177, 179, 193, 196, 254, 275, 307, 330–1, 365, 443, 456.

13   *WS*, XVI 181; *BV*, 243; *Par.*, 343 and 349; *Tatler*, 1709, No.52 referring to Wren under the pseudonym "Nestor".

14   cp. *supra* cap VIII, n. 14.

15   *WS*, XVIII 9, VII 228; *Par.*, 349

16   J. Lang, op. cit., 181; J. P. Malcolm, *Anecdotes of the Manners and Customs of London*, London, 1811, I 392.

17   cp. P. Howard, *The Royal Palaces*, Hamish Hamilton, London, 1970, 70.

18   *Hist. MSS. Comm.*, House of Lords, 1671–88, 16.

19   *WS*, IV 69.

20   *WS*, XIV x and XVIII 181–2; but cp. J. R. Clarke, *Was Sir Christopher Wren a Freemason?* in *Trans. of the Quattuor Coronati Lodge*, No. 2076 vol. 78 (1965) 201–6 (to whom I am grateful for co-operation); F. de P. Castells, *Was Sir Christopher Wren a Mason?*, Kemsing, London, 1917; V. Fürst, op. cit., 182, n. 32; E. F. Sekler, op. cit., 183.

21   cp. C. Weaver, *The Complete Building Accounts of the City Churches (Parochial) designed by Sir Christopher Wren*, in *Archaeologia* LXVI and *Par.*, 343–4.

22   J. Ward, op. cit., 95–111; H. A. L. Fisher, op. cit., cap. VII.

23   *Par.*, xi; A. Cunningham, *Lives of the Most Eminent British Painters Sculptors and Architects*, Murray, London, 1831, IV 147; V. Fürst, op. cit., 135; E. F. Sekler, op. cit., 26.

Appendix A

1 *WS*, XII 23 and XIV 152, pl. lxxiii for Oliver's engraving.

2 cp. J. Summerson, *Architecture*, op. cit., 256–7, pl. 208.

3 *WS*, XIII 54; D. Piper, op. cit., 344.

4 *WS*, VII 225–9.

5 *WS*, XVII 58–64, pl. lviii–lxiv; *Country Life*, 24 August 1951.

6 *WS*, XII 21, pl. xlix.

7 *WS*, XI 22–3.

8 cp. E. H. Pearse, *Christ's Hospital*, London, 1908, 151; *WS*, XI 60–80. cp. Letter of Wren on drawing as a subject for schools in *WS*, XI 74; E. F. Sekler, op. cit., 151.

9 *WS*, XI 84 ff, pl. liii–liv.

10 cp. Tighe and Davis, *Annals of Windsor*, Longman, London, 1858.

11 *WS*, XI 51–3 and XII, pl. xxii.

12 R. Plot, op. cit., 269; *WS*, XIX 57, pl. xv–xxiv. Plot was Secretary to the Royal Society when Wren was its President.

13 *WS*, X, pl. xv–xviii.

14 *WS*, XIX 148.

15 cp. R. Gunnis on *A Storm about a Pew* in *Bedfordshire Mag.*, II no. 15, 1950–51.

16 cp. *London Survey* XX 23 n., pl. 8–9.

17 W. H. St J. Hope, *History of Windsor Castle*, Country Life, London, 1912, II 386.

18 *PRO* MPA 41.

19 cp. *Vestry Minutes* for 13 January 1681/2 in Westminster City Library.

20 *WS*, X 58–60.

21 *Guildhall* library, MS 2461; *PRO*, 82/2441, 30 June 1673 and *MPA* 22.

22 *WS*, XIX p. xiv; Hugh Jones, *Present State of Virginia*, 1724, 26.

SELECT BIBLIOGRAPHY

SELECT BIBLIOGRAPHY

BOOKS:

ARKELL W. J. *Oxford Stone*, Faber, London, 1947
AUBREY J. *Brief Lives*, (ed. A. Powell) Cresset, London, 1949
—— *Miscellanies*, London, 1696
BELL W. G. *The Great Fire of London*, John Lane, London, 1920
BIRCH G. H. *London Churches of the 17th and 18th Centuries*, Batsford, London, 1896
BIRCH T. *History of the Royal Society*, Royal Society, London, 1753
BLOMFIELD R. *Six Architects*, Macmillan, London, 1933
BOLTON G. *Sir Christopher Wren*, Hutchinson, London, 1956
BRIGGS M. S. *Christopher Wren*, Falcon, London, 1951
—— *Wren, the Incomparable*, Allen & Unwin, London, 1953
BRYANT A. W. M. *King Charles II*, Collins, London, 1946
—— *Letters, Speeches and Declarations of Charles II*, Collins, London, 1935
BUMPUS J. S. *St Paul's Cathedral*, Treasure House, London, 1908
CARÖE W. D. *Tom Tower, Oxford*, OUP, Oxford, 1923
CASTELLS F. de P. *Was Sir Christopher Wren a Mason?* Kemsing, London, 1917
COBB G. *The Old Churches of London*, Batsford, London, 1942
COLVIN H. M. *Biographical Dictionary of English Architects 1660–1840*, Murray, London, 1954
CROWTHER J. G. *Founders of British Science*, Cresset, London, 1960
CUNNINGHAM A. *Lives of the Most Eminent British Painters, Sculptors and Architects*, Murray, London, 1833
DAVISON T. R. *Wren's City Churches*, The Builder, London, 1923
DEAN C. G. T. *The Royal Hospital Chelsea*, Hutchinson, London, 1950
— *Dictionary of National Biography*, Smith Elder, London
DOWNES K. *Christopher Wren*, Penguin, London, 1971
—— *Hawksmoor*, Thames & Hudson, London, 1969
DUGDALE W. *The History of St Paul's Cathedral in London*, (ed. H. Ellis) London, 1818
DUTTON R. *The Age of Wren*, Batsford, London, 1951
ELMES J. *Memoirs of the Life and Works of Sir Christopher Wren*, Priestley & Weale, London, 1823
—— *Sir Christopher Wren and His Times*, London, 1852

'ESPINASSE M. *Robert Hooke*, Heinemann, London, 1956

L'ESTRANGE A. G. *Greenwich Palace and Hospital*, Hurst & Blackett, London, 1886

EVELYN J. *Diary, 1637–1706*, (ed. E. S. de Beer) OUP, Oxford, 1955

—— *Fumifugium*, OUP, Oxford, 1930

—— *London Redivivum*, (ed. E. S. de Beer) OUP, Oxford, 1938

FABER H. *Caius Gabriel Cibber*, OUP, Oxford, 1926

FIENNES C. *Journeys Through England*, (ed. C. Morris) Cresset, London, 1949

FISHER H. A. L. *Pages from the Past*, (cap VII) OUP, Oxford, 1939

FÜRST V. *The Architecture of Sir Christopher Wren*, Lund Humphries, London, 1956

GOTCH J. A. *Inigo Jones*, Methuen, London, 1928

GREEN B. D. *Grinling Gibbons*, Methuen, London, 1964

GUNNIS R. T. *Achitecture of Sir Roger Pratt*, OUP, Oxford, 1928

—— *Early Science in Oxford*, OUP, Oxford, 1923

HALL A. R. *From Galileo to Newton*, Collins, London, 1963

HARTLIB S. *The Reformed Commonwealth of Bees*, London, 1665

HOOKE R. *Diary 1672–80*, (ed. H. W. Taylor, Francis Robinson and W. Adams) London, 1935

HOPKINS E. J. and RIMBAULT E. F. *The Organ, its History and Construction*, London, 1855

KNOOP D. and JONES G. F. *The London Mason in the 17th Century*, Manchester University Press, Manchester, 1935

LANG J. *Rebuilding of St Paul's after the Great Fire of London*, OUP, Oxford, 1956

LAW E. P. A. *The History of Hampton Court*, Bell, London, 1885–91

LINDSEY J. *Wren His Work and His Time*, Rich & Cowan, London, 1951

LOFTIE W. J. *Inigo Jones and Wren*, Rivington, London, 1893

LONGMAN W. *Three Cathedrals of St Paul*, London, 1873

MATTHEWS W. R. *A History of St Paul's Cathedral*, Phoenix, London, 1957

MILMAN H. H. *Annals of St Paul's*, London, 1869

MILMAN L. *Sir Christopher Wren*, Duckworth, London, 1908

—— *Names from the Dead*, OUP, Oxford, 1651

NORTH R. *Lives of the Norths*, (ed. A. Jessop) Bohn, London, 1890

PEPYS S. *Diary*, (ed. H. B. Wheatley) Bell, London, 1952

PEVSNER N. *Buildings of England, London I & II*, Penguin, London, 1957

—— *An Outline of European Architecture*, Penguin, London, 1945

PHILLIMORE L. *Sir Christopher Wren, His Family and Times*, Kegan Paul, London, 1881

PIPER D. *The Companion Guide to London*, Collins, London, 1964

PLOT R. *Natural History of Oxfordshire*, OUP, Oxford, 1677

POWELL A. *John Aubrey and His Friends*, Eyre & Spottiswoode, London, 1948

PURVER R. M. *The Royal Society, Concept and Creation*, Royal Society, London, 1967

RASMUSSEN S. E. *London, the Unique City*, Cape, London, 1948

REDDAWAY T. F. *The Rebuilding of London after the Great Fire*, Cape, London, 1951

RENDEL H. S. GOODHART *Nicholas Hawksmoor*, Benn, London, 1923

SEKLER E. K. *Wren and His Place in European Architecture*, Faber, London, 1956

SITWELL S. *British Architects and Craftsmen*, Batsford, London, 1945

SPRAT T. *The History of the Royal Society of London for the Improving of Natural Knowledge*, Royal Society, London, 1702

STIMSON D. *Scientists and Amateurs*, Sigma, London, 1949

STRATTON A. *The Life, Work and Influence of Sir Christopher Wren*, Liverpool University Press, Liverpool, 1897

SUMMERSON J. *Architecture in Britian 1530–1830*, Penguin, London, 1969

—— *Heavenly Mansions*, Cresset, London, 1949

—— *Sir Christopher Wren*, Collins, London, 1954

TIPPING H. A. *Grinling Gibbons and the Woodwork of his Age*, Country Life, London, 1914

WARD W. *Lives of the Professors of Gresham College*, London, 1740

WEAVER L. *Sir Christopher Wren*, Country Life, London, 1923

WEBB G. F. *Sir Christopher Wren*, Duckworth, London, 1937

WHINNEY M. *Wren*, Thames & Hudson, London, 1971

WHINNEY M. and O. MILLAR *English Art 1625–1714*, OUP, Oxford, 1957

WHITTAKER-WILSON G. *Sir Christopher Wren*, Methuen, London, 1932

WILLIS R. and CLARK J. W. *Architectural History of the University of Cambridge*, CUP, Cambridge, 1896

WREN S. *Parentalia or Memoirs of the Family of the Wrens*, London, 1750

Wren Society *Publications*, (ed. A. T. Bolton and H. D. Hendry) 20 vols., OUP, Oxford, 1929–43

WRIGHT-HENDERSON P. A. *The Life and Times of John Wilkins*, OUP, Oxford, 1910

ARTICLES:

ABERCROMBIE P. *Wren's Plan for London* in *Town Planning Review* X 1923–24, 71.

ADSHEAD S. D. *Sir Christopher Wren and his Plan for London* in *BV*, 161–74.

BATTEN M. I. *The Architecture of Robert Hooke* in *Walpole Soc.* XXV (1937).

BELL W. G. *The Rebuilding of London after the Great Fire* in *RIBA Jnl.* XLVII (1918).

BOLTON A. T. *Winchester Palace* in *RIBA Jnl.* XXXIII (1929–30) 43.

CHANCELLOR E. B. and TANNER L. *Wren's Restoration of Westminster Abbey* in *Connoisseur* LXXVII (1927) July.

CLARK S. *Observations on Wren's System of Buttresses* in *BV*, 73–82.

COLVIN H. M. *Roger North and Christopher Wren* in *Arch. Rev.* CX (1951) 257–60.

DAVIDGE W. R. *London's Bygone Building Acts* in *RIBA Jnl.* (3rd ser.) XXI 333–69.

GOTCH J. A. *Christopher Wren from the Personal Side* in *BV*, 9–30.

HAMILTON S. B. *The Place of Sir Christopher Wren in the History of Structural Engineering* in *Trans. of the Newcomen Soc.* XIV (1933–4) 27–42.

JONES H. W. *Wren and Natural History* in *Notes & Records of the Royal Society* XIII Vol. 1, 1958.

KEEN A. *Sir Christopher Wren's Parish Churches* in *BV*, 31–44.

KRANTZ J. C. *The Friendship of Boyle and Wren* in *Bull. of Hist. of Medicine* VIII (1939) 972–3.

LYNTON N. *A Wren Drawing for St Paul's* in *Burlington Mag.* XCVII (1955) 40–4.

MACARTNEY M. E. *Some Recent Investigations at St Paul's* in *BV*, 69–72.

MINNS E. H. and WEBB M. *Pembroke College Chapel* in *BV*, 229–32.

PEVSNER N. *Wren* in *Proceedings of the Royal Institution*, XXXV, 1954.
—— *The Term Architect in the Middle Ages* in *Speculum* XVII (1942) 549–62.

PITE A. B. *The Design of St Paul's Cathedral* in *BV*, 45–68.

RICHARDSON A. E. *Sir Christopher Wren's Public Buildings* in *BV*, 115–60.

STIMSON D. *Wren as F.R.S.* in *Scientific Mthly.* LIII (1941).

STRATTON A. *Dutch Influence on the Architecture of Sir Christopher Wren* in *BV*, 175–92.

SUMMERSON J. *Drawings for the London City Churches* in *RIBA Jnl.* (3rd ser.) LIX No. 4.
——*The Penultimate Design for St Paul's* in *Burlington Mag.* CIII, March 1961, 83–9.

TANNER L. *Wren's Restoration of Westminster Abbey* in *Connoisseur* LXXVII (1927).

WARREN E. P. *Sir Christopher Wren and the Repair of the Divinity School in BV*, 233–8.

WEAVER L. *Building Accounts of the City Churches* in *Archaeologia* LXVI.

WHINNEY M. *Wren's Visit to Paris* in *Gazette des Beaux Arts* II (1958) 229–42.

INDEX

Compiled by H. E. Crowe